WITHDRAWN

THE FABRICS OF HAWAII
(BARK CLOTH)

THE FABRICS OF HAWAII (BARK CLOTH)

by
ADRIENNE L. KAEPPLER

Anthropologist
Bernice Pauahi Bishop Museum, Honolulu

F. LEWIS, PUBLISHERS, LIMITED
PUBLISHERS BY APPOINTMENT TO THE LATE QUEEN MARY
LEIGH-ON-SEA

PRINTED AND MADE IN ENGLAND

©
Copyright by
F. Lewis, Publishers, Limited
The Tithe House
Leigh-on-Sea, Essex, England
SBN 85317 036 3

First Published 1975

PRODUCED UNDER THE SUPERVISION OF THE PUBLISHER, AT
THE DAEDALUS PRESS, STOKE FERRY, NORFOLK

Table of Contents

Acknowledgments – – – – – –	6
Introduction – – – – – –	7
References – – – – – –	15
Illustrations, 1-55 – – – – – –	17

Acknowledgments

The author and publishers wish to express their thanks and indebtedness to those who, in various ways, have given the valuable assistance that has made this record possible. Special thanks are due to the Director of the Bernice P. Bishop Museum, Honolulu, and to Mr. Peter Gilpin for his excellent photographs, without whose co-operation this book would have been impossible.

Introduction

*Their cloth ... is painted in a variety of patterns,
with a comprehensiveness and regularity of
design that bespeaks infinite taste and fancy.*

THUS WROTE Captain James King in March, 1779, during the third voyage of Captain Cook.* This infinite taste and fancy, as well as the novelty of making cloth out of bark, was well recognized by Cook himself, his officers, and men. Scores of pieces of bark cloth from Polynesia were taken to England on Cook's three voyages and have subsequently found their way to many parts of the world. Most of these 18th-century bark cloths have been cut into smaller and smaller pieces, until what remains today can best be described as 'samples' – many of which were bound into books.

The most systematic of such volumes of bark cloth pieces was a group arranged by Alexander Shaw which included a printed introduction 'with a particular account of the manner and manufacturing the same in the various Islands of the South Seas,' published in 1787. It is not known how many of these *Catalogues of the different specimens of cloth collected in the three voyages of Captain Cook* were actually compiled and circulated; however, there are about 30 of these volumes known today. In the *Catalogues* in this series that I have examined, the actual bark cloth specimens do not agree with the published list included with the introduction, nor is there consistency from *Catalogue* to *Catalogue*. Although reputedly from the three voyages of Cook, the largest number of bark cloth pieces is always from Hawaii, which was visited only on the third voyage. Shaw, too, must have recognized the infinite taste and fancy demonstrated by the Hawaiians and much of our knowledge of 18th-century Hawaiian bark cloth comes from these *Catalogues*.

A number of other 'manuscript' volumes of bark cloth pieces (that is, without a printed introduction or list) were also compiled in the late 18th and early 19th centuries, and each of these is unique. Some of these seem to have been compiled by owners of museums and private collections of the time, such as one now in the Peabody Museum, Salem, Massachusetts, which came from the London Museum of William Bullock, sold at auction in 1819. This paper-covered collection includes 22 bark cloth pieces, 20 of which are Hawaiian (see Kaeppler, 1974, p. 92). At least two other volumes of bark

---

* Cook and King, 1784, Vol. III, p. 148-149.

cloth pieces are bound in parchment covers and may have come from the Leverian Museum of London which was sold at auction in 1806 (see Kaeppler, in preparation). But the most important of these early compilations, from the point of view of 18th-century bark cloth design, is a bound volume now in Bishop Museum. This includes 110 bark cloth pieces approximately eight by ten inches in size, many of which are Hawaiian. Twenty-three of these are reproduced here in actual size. These pieces are considerably larger than those included in the Shaw *Catalogues* and other known books of samples from the 18th century, and thus impart a more accurate notion of the organization of design elements. It is not known when or by whom this volume was compiled, although by tradition the pieces are said to have come from Cook's voyages. There can be little question, however, that most of the pieces are of 18th-century manufacture.

Because most surviving 18th-century bark cloth pieces from Hawaii have been cut into small pieces it is difficult to tell today what the overall organization of the design elements was, but it is quite certain that the organization was considerably different from much of the design organization of 19th-century bark cloth. Large collections of 19th-century pieces can be found in the Arning collection in the Museum für Völkerkunde, Berlin; the Peabody Museum, Salem, Massachusetts; and especially in the extensive collection in the Bishop Museum, Honolulu.

In this essay and the accompanying plates we attempt to illustrate the infinite taste and fancy of Hawaiian bark cloth design in both the 18th and 19th centuries. Although the manufacture of Hawaiian bark cloth is no longer a living tradition, the designs have become a profound source of inspiration in the renaissance of Hawaiian ethnic identity and should be known to artists of all nations. It is a truism that standards of taste and aesthetic systems change over time, but it is often tacitly assumed that such changes take place more slowly in nonliterate cultures. Thus, it is illuminating in this regard to follow the changes that took place in Hawaiian bark cloth design during less than one hundred years. Much of the impetus for these changes was certainly owing to contact with the Western world, but it should be pointed out that this change was not a simple linear one that can be characterized by the oversimplified concept of 'European acculturation'. Rather, the change can be more aptly characterized as *evolution* along indigenous lines. Indeed, the change is similar in some ways to the impact of China on European art. For although it is easy to isolate Chinese forms and motifs, the basic underlying structure is still European. The result may be quite specific such as Chinese Chippendale or more generalized as in the concept of Chinoiserie. Similarly, just as one can isolate European-inspired motifs in Hawaiian bark cloth and the evidence of imported metal tools on the beaters and design stamps, the basic underlying concepts are still Hawaiian.

Simply stated, 18th-century Hawaiian bark cloth is relatively thick, is often ribbed, and has bold angular designs, while 19th-century bark cloth is thinner, has smaller designs organized differently, occasionally includes circular motifs, and has an elaboration of the watermark which is found only incipiently on 18th-century bark cloth. There was, however, little change in the manufacturing process itself.

The finest Hawaiian bark cloth (*kapa*) in both pre-European times and in the 19th century was made from the inner bark of the paper mulberry tree (*Broussonetia papyrifera*), known as *wauke* in Hawaiian. Also used were *mamaki* (*Pipturus albidus*) and *'ulu* or breadfruit (*Artocarpus incisus*). The paper mulberry, however, was by far the most important and was cultivated specifically for making bark cloth. Planted from cuttings, the *wauke* was left to grow from one to two years to reach a height of two to three meters. During the growing period the side branches were carefully removed to eliminate holes in the final product. When the tree was cut the diameter was usually less than three centimeters. With a sharp shell the inner and outer bark was pulled from the stem. The outer bark was scraped away and discarded and the inner bark soaked in sea water to make it soft and clean. The beating process was in two stages – a preliminary beating with a round beater (*hohoa*) on a wooden anvil (or according to some, a stone anvil), and a second beating with a square beater (*i'e kuku*). During the first beating the inner bark was beaten into long strips. These strips were placed in bundles and soaked in water until they were soft. The macerated bundle was then beaten until the pieces were felted together to form one rectangular piece. It was then dried in the sun and bleached by spreading it over moss and exposing it to the night dew. If larger pieces were desired they were sewn with thread of twisted bark cloth or *hau* (*Hibiscus tiliaceus*). The cloth was then ready to be decorated.*

Decoration of Hawaiian *kapa* made extensive use of color and design. Dyes were made from charcoal, red and yellow ochers, a liquid obtained from the sea urchin (purple), and from various parts of plants – giving shades of red, brown, yellow, black, a pale blue, and a light green. The most usual combination, however, especially on 18th-century bark cloth, was a reddish brown and black on a yellowish or natural ground. Solid colors were obtained by completely immersing the finished piece of cloth in a bowl of dye or in a taro swamp, or by immersing the partly beaten strips in dye before the final beating. Alternately, the upper surface of the cloth might be brushed with dye if a background color other than natural was desired – this latter process being the more usual one in 18h-century *kapa*. Design was of two quite different sorts. One kind of design, a 'watermark', was impressed into the cloth during the second beating and a second design was applied to the upper surface of the finished cloth. Thus, it is proper to speak of two layers of design in Hawaiian *kapa*, both of which reached their fullest expression during the 19th century.

---

* For more detail on process of manufacture see Brigham, 1911; Buck, 1957; and Kooijman, 1972.

Impressed Designs

The first layer of design which permeates the whole piece of cloth is characterized by the use of watermarks and grooves. Grooving or ribbing, done by pushing the dampened cloth into the grooves of a special wooden board, appears to be a technique that was used exclusively in the 18th century and was unique to Hawaii.* Both sides of a special board were completely carved in close parallel grooves – the grooves of the two sides being carved in different widths. The cloth was pushed into the grooves with a carved wooden implement, or, it is said, with a pig's jawbone. Such cloth is usually rather thick and the grooves impart a certain amount of pliability and elasticity which would be especially useful in garments that require tight wrapping such as the loin cloth, *malo*.

Watermarks in fine lines either in one direction or crossed at right or oblique angles are occasionally distinguishable on a few bark cloth pieces collected in Hawaii on Cook's third voyage. These watermarks were impressed into the cloth during the final beating with a beater carved with parallel grooves. The watermark which resulted is similar to that found on fine bark cloth from Tahiti in 18th-century collections, which was also finished with a beater carved in fine parallel grooves. Unfortunately, no *i'e kuku*, second stage beaters, are found in Hawaiian collections from Cook's third voyage, so we have no firsthand evidence of how the beaters were made during the 1770's.† An *i'e kuku* said to have been collected on Vancouver's voyage to Hawaii in 1792-1795 (and now in Canterbury Museum, Christchurch, New Zealand) has parallel grooves, and the four faces are cross-hatched. Thus we know that by the end of the 18th century, at least straight and cross-hatched lines were carved into the second stage beaters, but it would appear that beaters were not extensively carved until the introduction of European metal nails made such carving more feasible. Although straight lines are relatively easy to carve with a shark's tooth or similar tool, the intricate carving on extant 19th-century beaters, which were undoubtedly carved with metal tools, indicates that Hawaiian craftsmen were quick to recognize that the new metal tools could be easily adapted to their traditional techniques. A whole series of elaborate designs developed and an efflorescence of watermarked *kapa* was stimulated.

Watermarks from intricately carved beaters have traditionally been thought to be the

---

* Brigham, following the registration information on a piece of bark cloth in the Museum für Völkerkunde, Vienna, attributes a grooved piece to Tonga (1911, color plate Y), but this is surely incorrect (as is some of the information about the origin of the Vienna collection). For recent work on the Vienna collection see Kaeppler, (in preparation).

† A *hohoa*, first stage beater, is in the Cook collection in Leningrad.

most important distinguishing feature of traditional Hawaiian bark cloth. But an examination of pieces traceable to the 18th century, and particularly those taken to England on Cook's third voyage, demonstrate that such watermarking is not a prominent feature. Rather, the presence of elaborate watermarks seems to indicate 19th-century manufacture and helps to distinguish these later pieces from those made in pre-European times. Introduction of metal tools appear to have stimulated makers of *i'e kuku* beaters to greater 'artmanship' and the makers of *kapa* to concentrate on fine quality cloth that would show the watermarks to their best advantage. Indeed, the production of intricately carved *i'e kuku* beaters may have become an end in itself, and the beater treated much as an art object. A number of such beautifully carved beaters in the collection of the Bishop Museum seem to have been used little, if at all, and some of the frequently carved intricate beater designs are seldom found on extant *kapa*. Further, the bark cloth made with these beaters is so fine that much of it may have been made specifically as visual symbols of rank and prestige rather than for functional clothing or bed covers—introduced woven textiles and blankets having replaced the pre-European uses of bark cloth. These new extremely fine kapas may have been used as prestigious gifts, for ceremonial wear, for the top decorative covers of European style beds, and as wrappings for the dead. Such *kapa* was also used to make European style dresses of the *mu'umu'u* 'Mother Hubbard' variety that hung straight from the shoulders and did not require wrapping, which would certainly have caused it to rip.

Designs on these carved beaters are predominantly angular and are often named after natural or cultural forms, such as the upper left example of plate 31, called *upena pupu*, which signifies net meshes enhanced with small circles. It is not known whether the carver of *i'e kuku* had such forms in mind when carving the designs, whether they were given names after they were carved because of their similarity to some other form, or whether the names were applied or elaborated by the first writers on the subject, such as the Hawaiian writer, S. M. Kamakau, or the museum curator, William T. Brigham. It is likely that each of these possibilities contributed to the elaborate naming system which now exists.* Watermarks can best be seen when the cloth is held up to the light and plates 30, 31, and 32 were photographed with back light to emphasize the watermark. In some cases, as in the upper left of plate 31, the printed design on the upper surface has all but disappeared. The upper surface design is still distinguishable in the examples on the lower right of plate 31 and the upper right of plate 32. The *kapa* depicted in plate 30 was found in a burial cave, probably of 19th-century origin, and may have been used as a wrapping for the dead. The eight examples in plates 31 and 32 are from 19th-century bed covers (*kapa moe*), skirts (*pa'u*), and shoulder coverings (*kihei*).

---

* See Buck (1957) for details.

The idea of impressing a watermark into the cloth may have given rise to an extension of this concept, that is, piercing the design completely through the cloth. This resulted in a lace-like perforated fabric (plate 33). The finished product is unique to Hawaii, but the technique of manufacture has never been satisfactorily explained. Its primary purpose may have been for overlaying (see p. 15 below). The design composition is often similar to the 18th-century use of the convergence of straight and diagonal linear elements in the painted surface designs (*e.g.*, plates 6 and 15).

Painted and Printed Designs
The second layer of design in Hawaiian bark cloth is that painted or printed on the upper surface. These designs are also considerably different in bark cloth from the 18th and 19th centuries, the former having bold, heavy designs while the latter have smaller, more regular and delicate designs in more limited or outlined design fields. Plates 1-24 depict bark cloth pieces from the 18th century; plates 25-29 are not traceable to the 18th century, but by their style they seem either to have been made in the 18th century, or to have retained 18th-century design concepts into the 19th century. Designs on the 18th-century *kapas* are predominantly straight lines in series which run parallel with the cloth and/or in various diagonals to it. These lines are often crossed by other straight or diagonal lines (plates 1-5) or the straight lines are met by other lines at a diagonal (plates 6 and 15). Parallel zigzag lines are often added to the straight lines (*e.g.*, plates 7 and 8); sometimes the lines are formed of dots (plates 9 and 10) or short wavy design elements (plate 11); or lines may be crossed to form diamonds (plates 12, 13, and 14). Lines were also combined into large diagonal forms (plates 15-19) and might incorporate large and small right angles as a prominent feature (plates 20-23). Occasionally several of these elements were combined (plate 24). In short, the overall design conceptualization appears to be based on creative combinations of linear elements that cross and converge to form squares, triangles, and diagonal forms, giving a feeling of boldness and directness.

Designs were executed with pieces of bamboo, According to Captain King on Cook's third voyage,

> The exactness with which the most intricate patterns are continued, is the more surprising, when we consider, that they have no stamps, and that the whole is done by the eye, with pieces of bamboo cane dipped in paint; the hand being supported by another piece of the cane, in the manner practiced by our painters.
> (*Cook and King, 1784, Vol. III, p. 149.*)

From this passage it appears that the bamboo was used as a pen and Captain Clerke's description emphasizes this,

> They dye their Cloth in a variety of fashions, and with such a degree of exactitude that we made no doubt but they must have contrived some method of printing it, however we several times saw them, during our stay, lay on the different colours by hand with an Instrument resembling a Pen made with a Reed, and found that constant practice had brought them to this degree of excellence, for that they had no idea of any other method.   (*Beaglehole, 1967, Part I, p. 594.*)

Unfortunately early accounts do not indicate if the 'pens' had single or multiple points. Single pointed pens may have been used to draw lines with the aid of a bamboo ruler, or the long edge of the 'pen' may have been used as a 'stamp' by dipping it into dye and pressing it on to the cloth. Multiple pointed pens may have been used to draw parallel lines or by using the long edges of the prongs as stamps. All of the designs in plates 1-27 could have been made with such lining tools – along with infinite skill and patience.

Contrast this 18th-century emphasis on linear elements with the 19th-century design conceptualization in which the designs are more consciously 'placed', and use negative space as part of the design. There is considerably less emphasis on linear elements, and the straight lines that do occur are more on the order of space dividers and give frames to enclosed arrangements of small motifs. Sometimes these frames are entirely filled in with one design (plates 34 and 35), or the linear elements may become part of an overall pattern (plate 36). More often, however, the linear elements enclose or define the space for the more consciously placed motifs (plates 37-41). Occasionally the linear elements disappear entirely (plate 42) and the motifs are placed only in relation to each other and negative space. Such designs have a rather 'modern' feeling from a Western point of view, abstracted as they are from their linear context. On the other hand, motifs were also combined in ways which may seem incongruous to a Western eye (plates 43 and 44).

Most of the designs on these 19th-century *kapas* were printed with stamps that were carved on the inside end section of strips of bamboo 12 to 18 inches in length. One end was carved with a long, narrow design (ranging in length from one to five inches and in width from one-tenth to eight-tenths of an inch) and the uncarved section functioned as a handle. The stamps were so skilfully placed in groups – either side to side or end to end – that the beginning and ending of each individual impression is sometimes difficult to detect. In plate 41, for example, the same long narrow stamp with 12 chevrons and four triangles is printed 17 times and a stamp of six carved diagonals is printed eight times. In several of the plates the individual stamp patterns can also be easily delineated. It appears that these intricately carved bamboo stamps were a 19th-century elaboration that evolved from combining indigenous motifs and bamboo pens under the influence of new tools made from European introduced iron. Consider for example, the similarities between the chevron designs of plates 23 and 41 (both reproduced here actual size). The 18th-century design in plate 23 is surely the prototype for the 19th-century design of plate 41. The former was painted freehand, while the latter, which was printed with a carved stamp, has more controlled regularity. Or compare the 18th-century freehand design of plate 12, probably executed with bamboo pen and ruler, with the corresponding motifs in plates 42 and 43. The diamond motif itself is surely an indigenous one, but a new regularity of motif repetition is introduced by the 19th-century stamp.

Although it is possible that some stamps carved on the inside of strips of bamboo did exist in pre-European times, none can be traced to collections from Cook's voyage. Indeed, Captain King denied that Hawaiians used stamps in decorating their bark cloth (see p. 12 above). It is more likely that single, and possibly multipronged, pens could also be used as stamps and that these furnished the prototype for the more elaborate 19th-century stamps. Furthermore, no pieces of bark cloth known to have come from Hawaii on Cook's third voyage include designs that would necessarily have been made with carved stamps, although some designs suggest that multipronged pens or 'liners' (as they are known today) were used either as pens or stamps. Carved stamps and multipronged liners abound in 19th-century collections and, of course, the extant 19th-century *kapas* were undoubtedly printed with such stamps and liners. It seems safe to conclude that Hawaiians quickly recognized the usefulness of metal tools and adopted them to carving stamps on bamboo strips that they had previously used mainly as pens. This resulted in an elaboration and refinement of their traditional motifs and techniques.

With new, more elaborate printing tools available, Hawaiian women evolved the new concepts of design organization outlined above and they elaborated them in yet other ways. Small design motifs from bamboo stamps were sometimes used to 'fill in' larger designs (plate 45) giving yet another, less obvious, dimension to the complete decoration. Only seldom do we find flat two-dimensionality (as in plate 46) without subtle, hidden dimensions in which Hawaiians typically took great delight. Just as in Hawaiian poetry, music, and dance, where levels of meaning were hidden in seemingly straightforward artistry, so the *kapa* maker hid some of her designs from first sight. For example, the immediate impression of the kapa depicted in plate 45 is that of a repetitious design of large triangles, three of which combine into a larger form, on a blue background. On closer examination one finds that each of the three triangles that make up one design is filled in with different small motifs. And furthermore, the watermark impressed from the beater is visible only when held to the light. *Kaona*, hidden meaning, is expressed with classic Hawaiian subtlety. Overall designs, such as those depicted in plates 47-51, find their subtlety in placement, color, and watermark, but the *pièce de resistance* of the Hawaiian artistic genius in two-dimensional design was surely the creation of motifs out of negative space, particularly in designs created from the unprinted parts of the cloth (plates 52 and 53). Here one simple stamp is printed over and over to form the 'background', while the design is formed from the unprinted parts of the cloth (plate 53), or the negative space between the stamps (plate 52).

Another result of European influence on bark cloth manufacture was the use of European motifs, especially 'calico' designs which must have been introduced by New England missionary wives. Such design transference was admired by Wilkes in his *Narrative of the United States Exploring Expedition,* which visited Hawaii in the early 1840's,

> They were all much struck with the dress of the native women, its unusual neatness and becoming appearance. It seemed remarkable that so many of them should be clothed in foreign manufacture, and that apparently of an expensive kind; but on closer examination, the dresses proved to be tapas, printed in imitation of merino shawls, ribands, etc.
>
> (*Wilkes, 1845, Vol. IV, pp. 71-72.*)

True imitations of European designs, however, are only seldom found on extant Hawaiian bark cloth, and it would appear that Hawaiians were quick to adapt any European borrowed motifs to their own canons of taste. Even those designs which apparently show European influence (plates 54 and 55) are still unmistakably Hawaiian.

Seemingly unique to Hawaii in bark cloth decoration was cord snapping, while overlaying was shared with Tahiti. Although it is probable that these processes were indigenous, it is likely that they continued to develop after European influence, for examples of Hawaiian bark cloth which appear to be prototypes for these techniques have been found in collections known to derive from Cook's third voyage. The former process is similar to that used by carpenters to make straight lines with chalk. Overlaying usually consists of pounding European cloth (often red in color) or colored bark cloth into an uncolored bark cloth sheet. It is possible that an indigenous technique was elaborated owing to the stimulus of the making of European style quilts. But whether these techniques were elaborated before or after European influence is really unimportant because, in either case, they demonstrate the inventiveness of the Hawaiians in using these techniques to decorate bark cloth, which was certainly not how they were used by Europeans. New techniques, concepts, and designs developed in post-European times were incorporated or creatively adapted into the Hawaiian aesthetic tradition and quickly became part of their constantly changing standards of taste. The efflorescence was not destined to endure. In less than a century after European contact, bark cloth manufacture in Hawaii was a thing of the past – leaving for future generations only a mute legacy of infinite taste and fancy.

References

Beaglehole, J. C. *The Journals of Captain Cook. Volume 3, The Voyage of the Resolution and Discovery.* Cambridge University Press, 1967.

Brigham, William T. 'Ka Hana Kapa: The Story of the Manufacture of Kapa (Tapa), or Bark-Cloth, in Polynesia and Elsewhere, but Especially in the Hawaiian Islands.' *Memoirs of the Bernice P. Bishop Museum*, 3:1-273, 1911. (Album of color plates appended.)

Buck, Peter H. (Te Rangi Hiroa). *Arts And Crafts of Hawaii.* Bernice P. Bishop Museum Special Publication 45. Honolulu, 1957.

Buhler, A. and Naumann, W. *Bark Cloths of the South Seas.* CIBA Review, Basle. No. 33, 1940.

Cook, James and King, James. *A Voyage to the Pacific Ocean.... In Three Volumes. Vol. I and II written by Captain James Cook, F.R.S. Vol. III by Captain James King, LL.D. and F.R.S.*, London, 1784.

Force, Roland W. and Maryanne. *Captain James Cook, Sis Ashton Lever, and Miss Sarah Stone*: incorporating *Art and Artifacts of the Eighteenth Century.* (To be published by Bishop Museum Press). *In preparation.*

Kaeppler, Adrienne L. 'Cook Voyage Provenance of the "Artificial Curiosities" of Bullock's Museum.' *Man* (N.S.) 9:68-92, 1974.

Kooijman, Simon. *Tapa in Polynesia.* Bernice P. Bishop Museum Bulletin 234. Honolulu, 1972.

Shaw, Alexander. *A catalogue of the different specimens of cloth collected in the three voyages of Captain Cook....* London, 1787.

Wilkes, C. *A Narrative of the United States Exploring Expedition during the years 1838-1842.* 5 volumes and atlas. Philadelphia, 1845.

Illustrations

Photographs by Peter Gilpin
(All specimens are from Bishop Museum Collections)

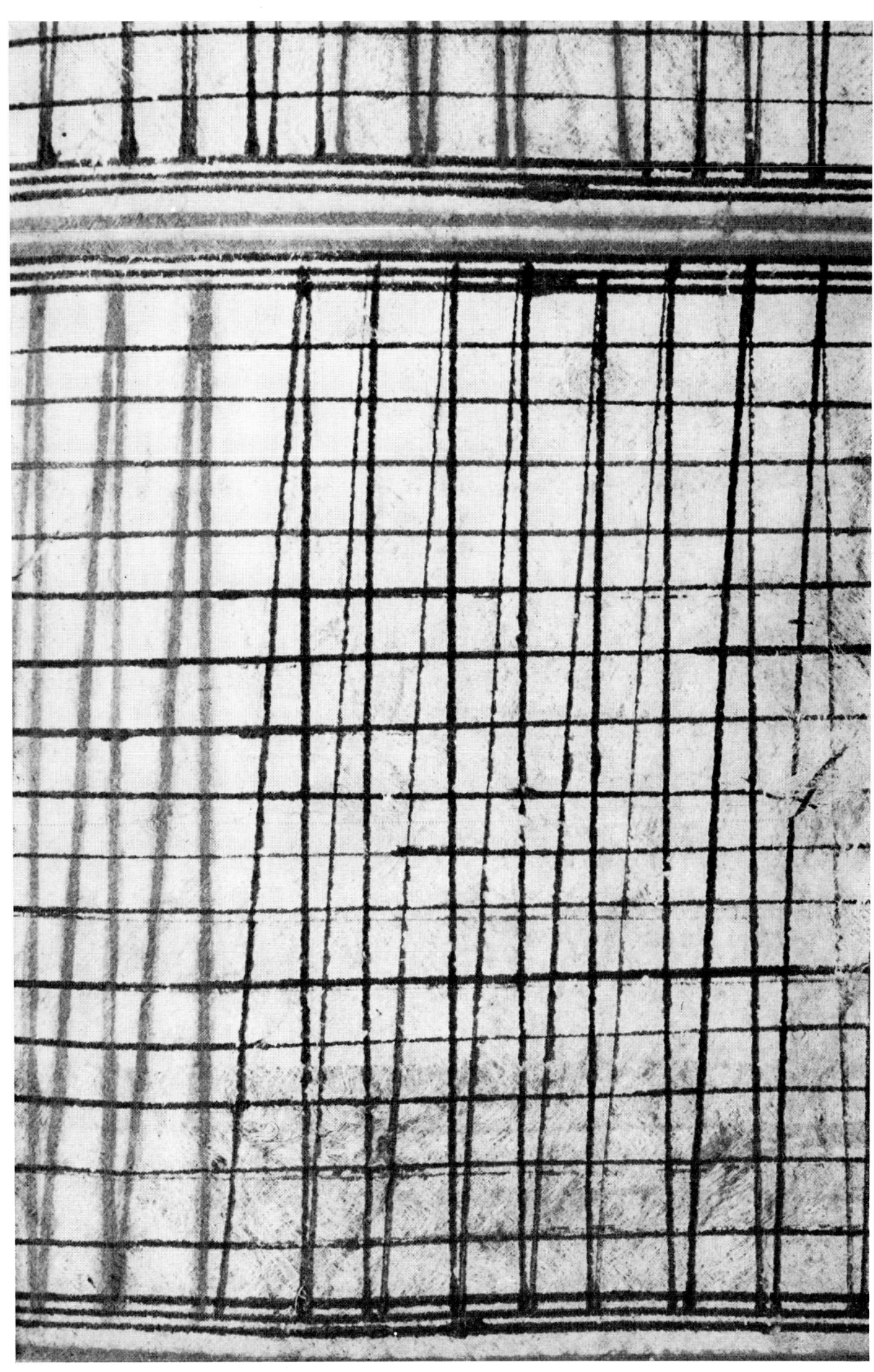

1. Reddish brown* and black lines on natural.
Bound volume, p. 12. Actual size.
* *Reddish brown in these descriptions is an inclusive term for various shades ranging from salmon to a dark red-brown.*

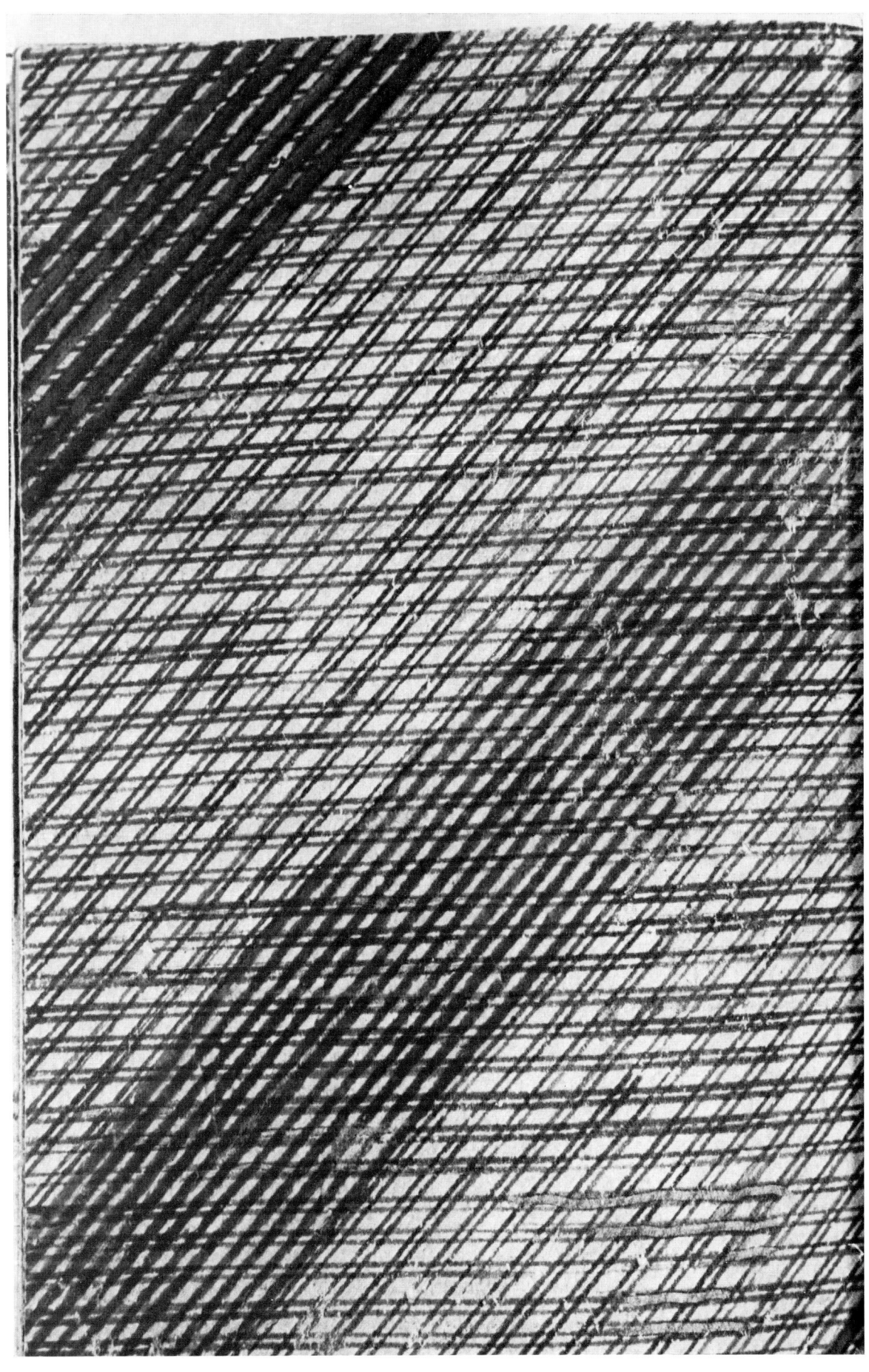

2. Reddish brown and black lines on natural.
Bound volume, p. 5. Actual size.

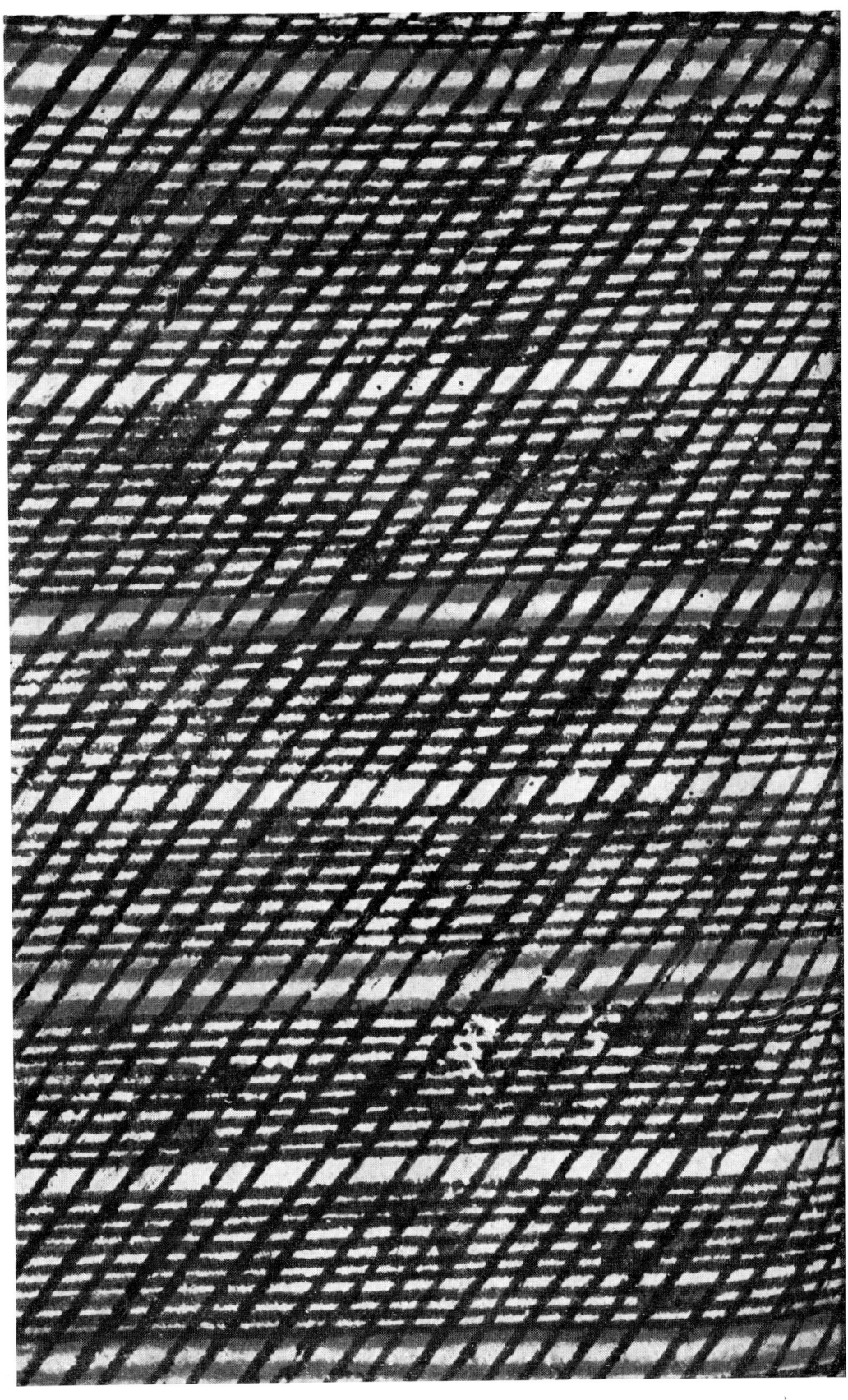

3. Reddish brown and black lines on natural.
Bound volume, p. 60. Actual size.

4. Reddish brown and black lines on natural.
    Bound volume, p. 75. Actual size.

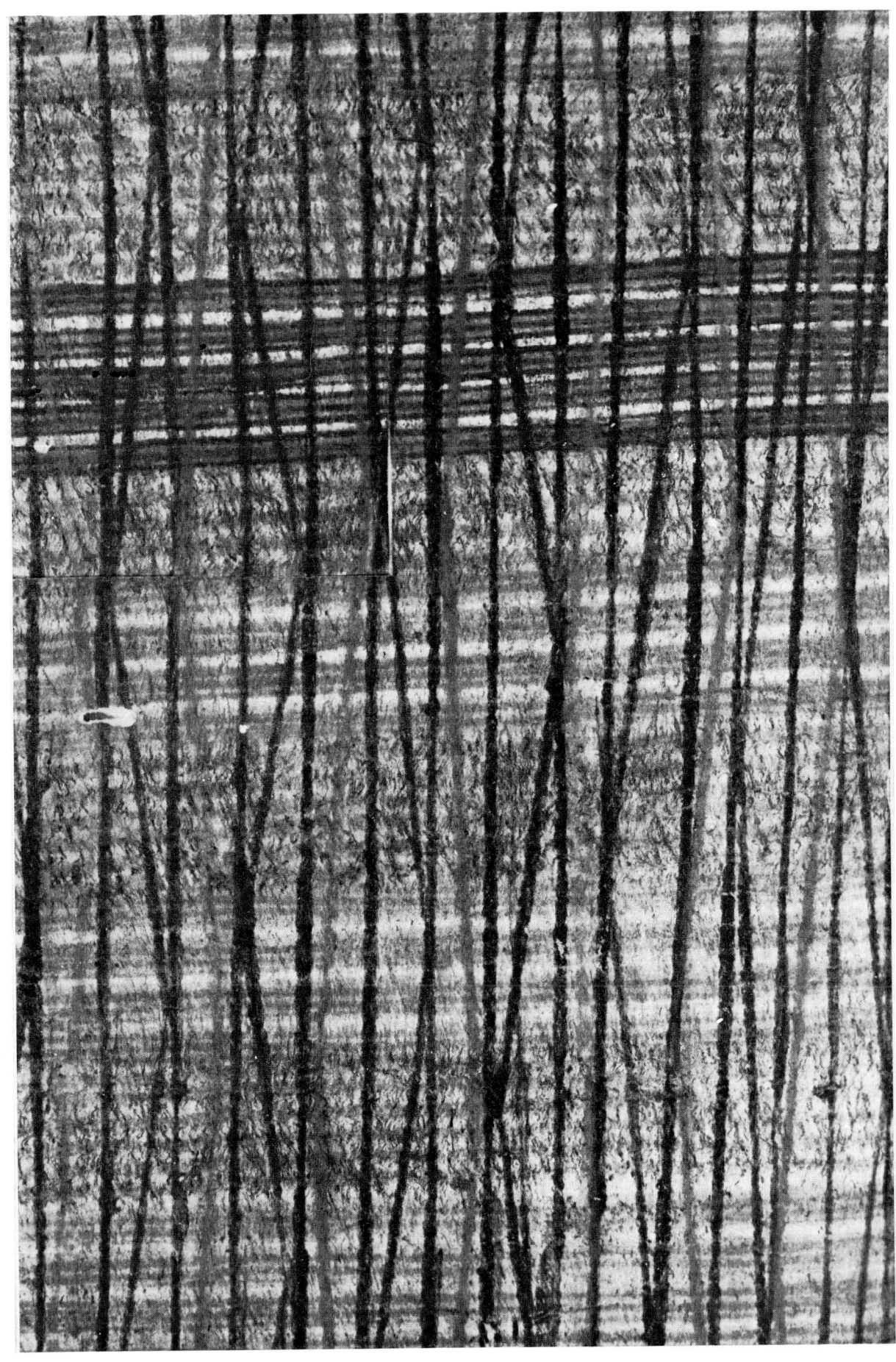

5. Reddish brown and black lines on brown and natural.
Bound volume, plate 23. Actual size.

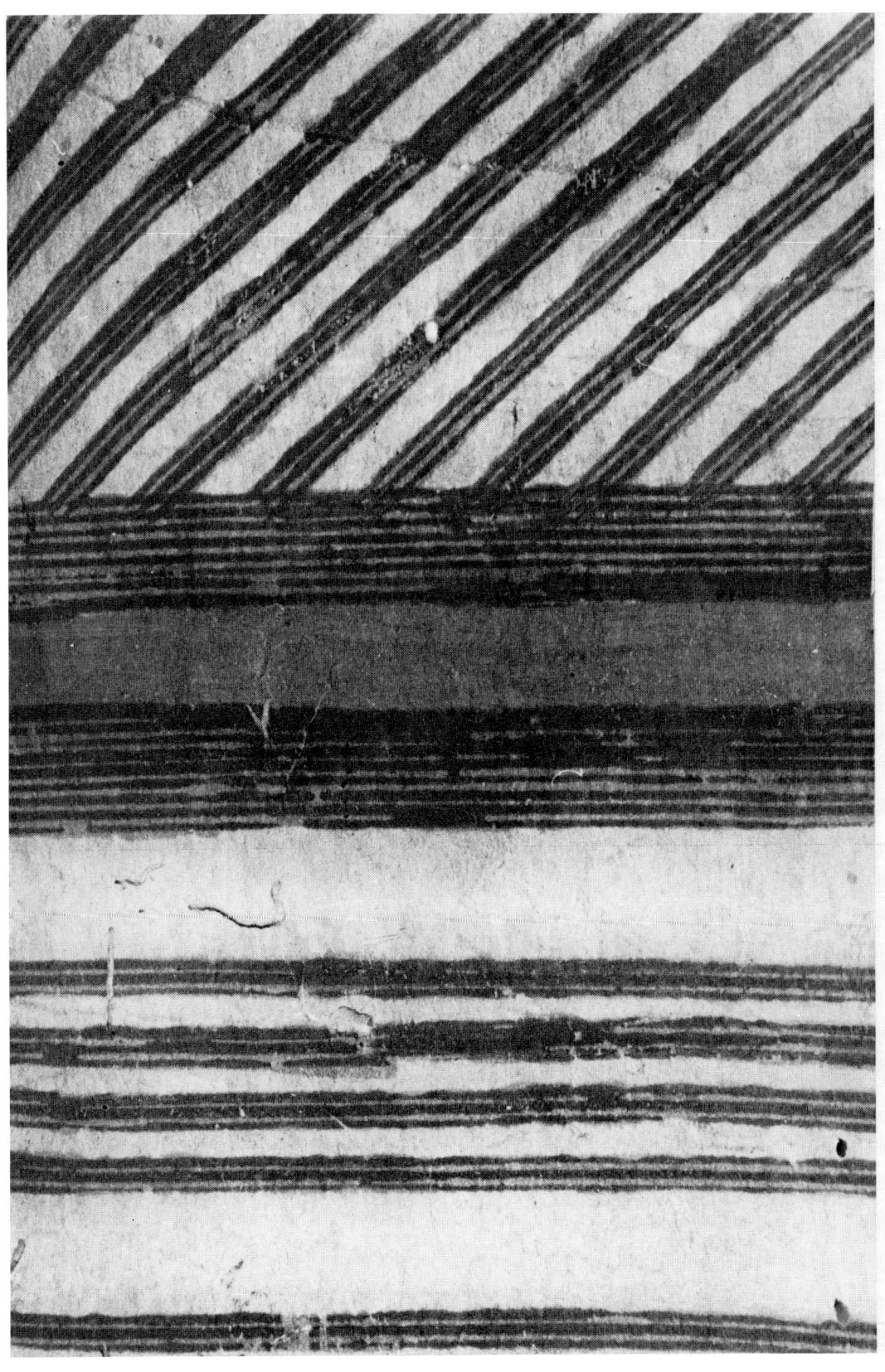

6. Reddish brown and black lines on natural. Bound volume, p. 84. Actual size.

7. Reddish brown and black on natural. Bound volume, p. 67. Actual size.

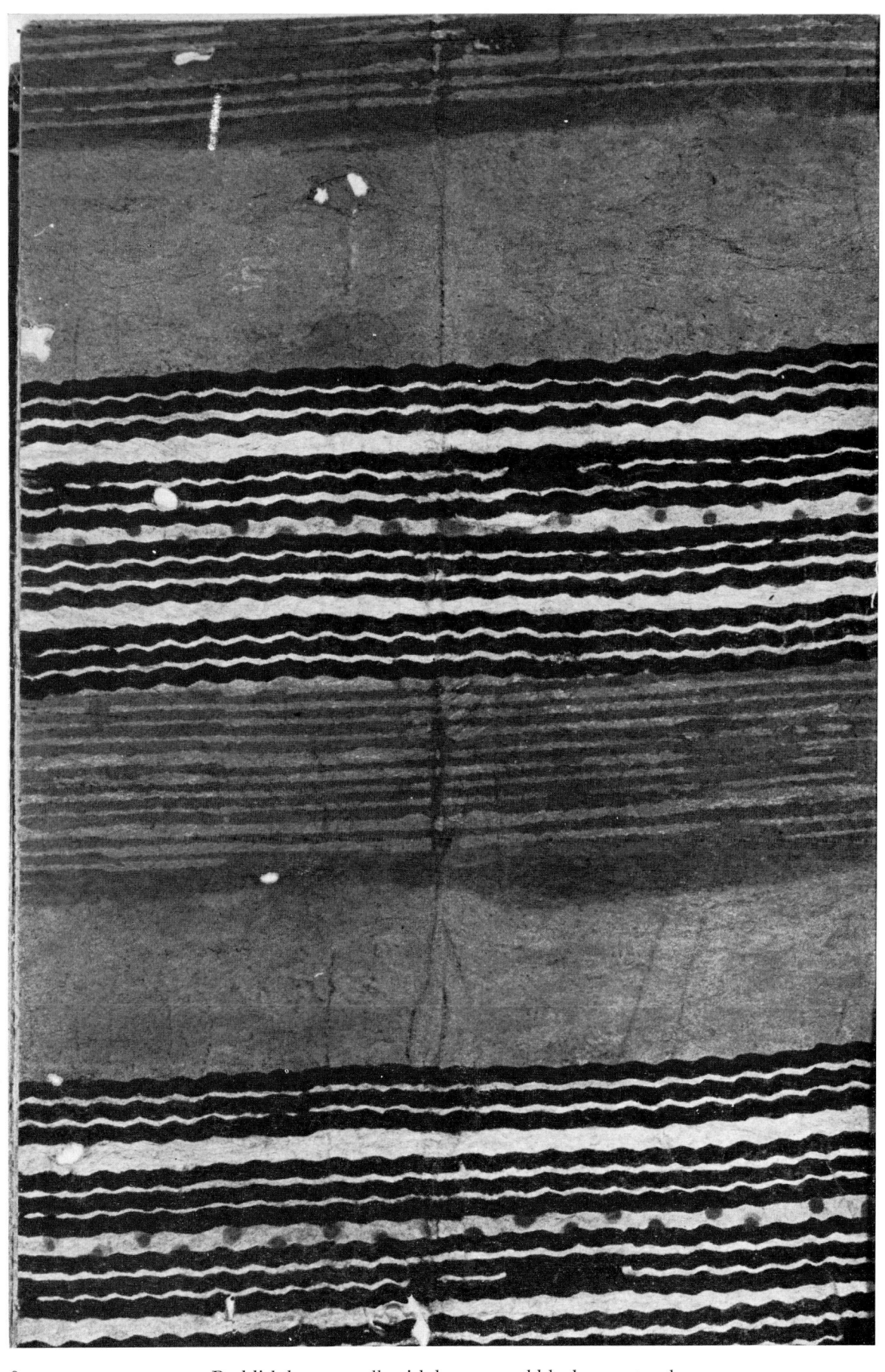

8. Reddish brown, yellowish brown, and black on natural.
Bound volume, p. 1. Actual size.

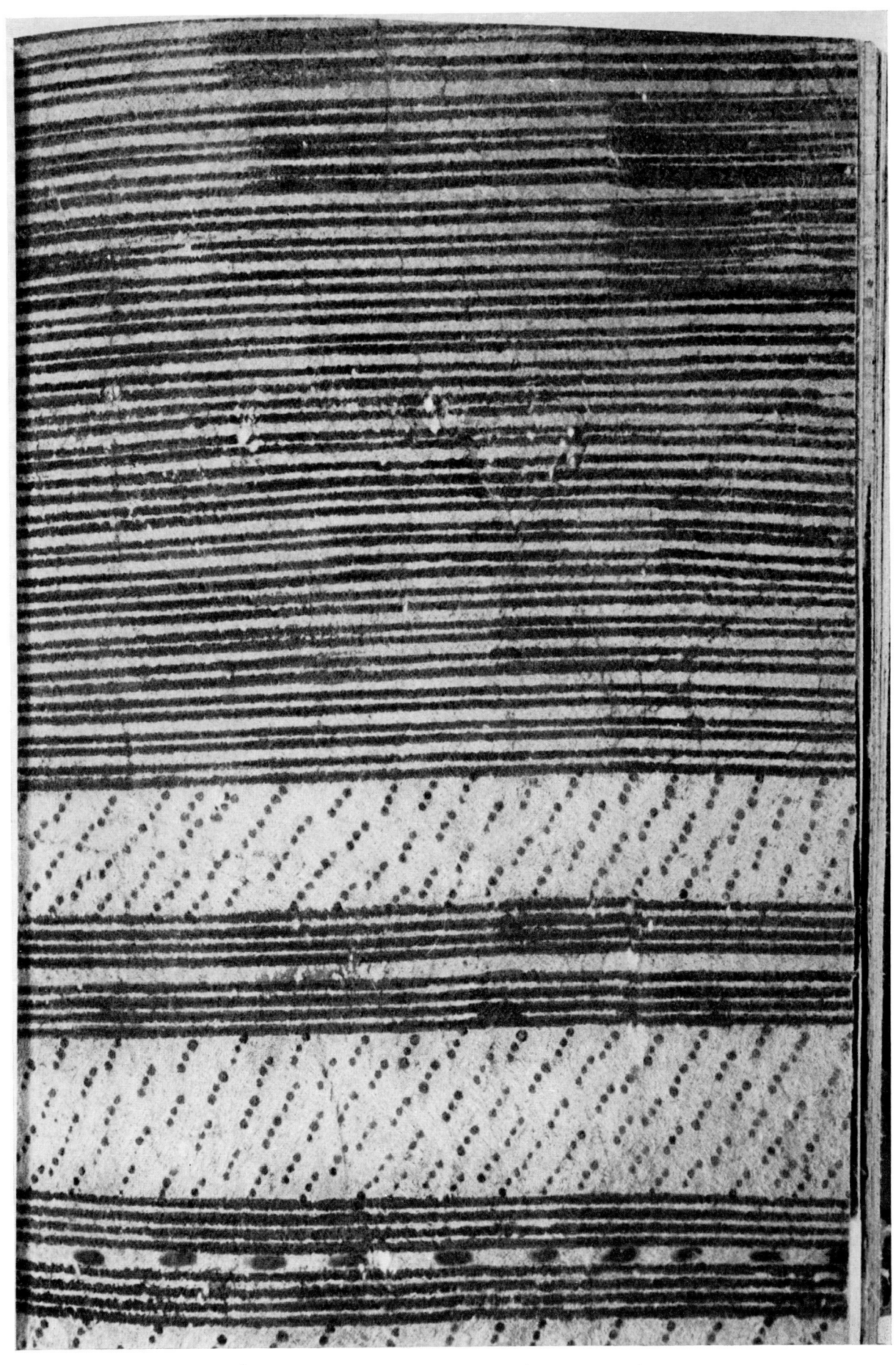

9. Black lines and reddish brown dots on natural.
Bound volume, p. 6. Actual size.

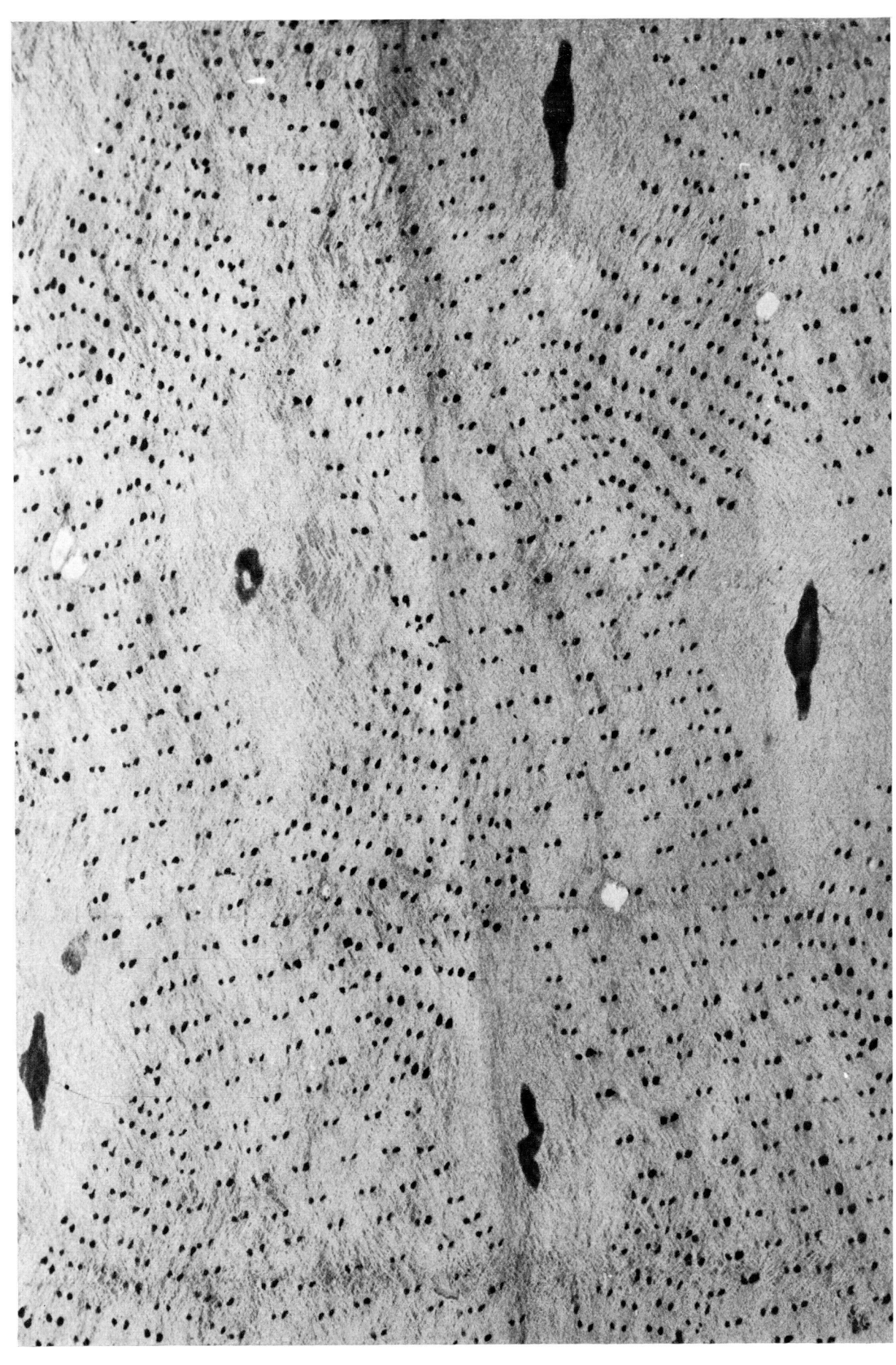

10. Black dots and red ochre figures on natural. Bound volume, p. 11. Actual size.

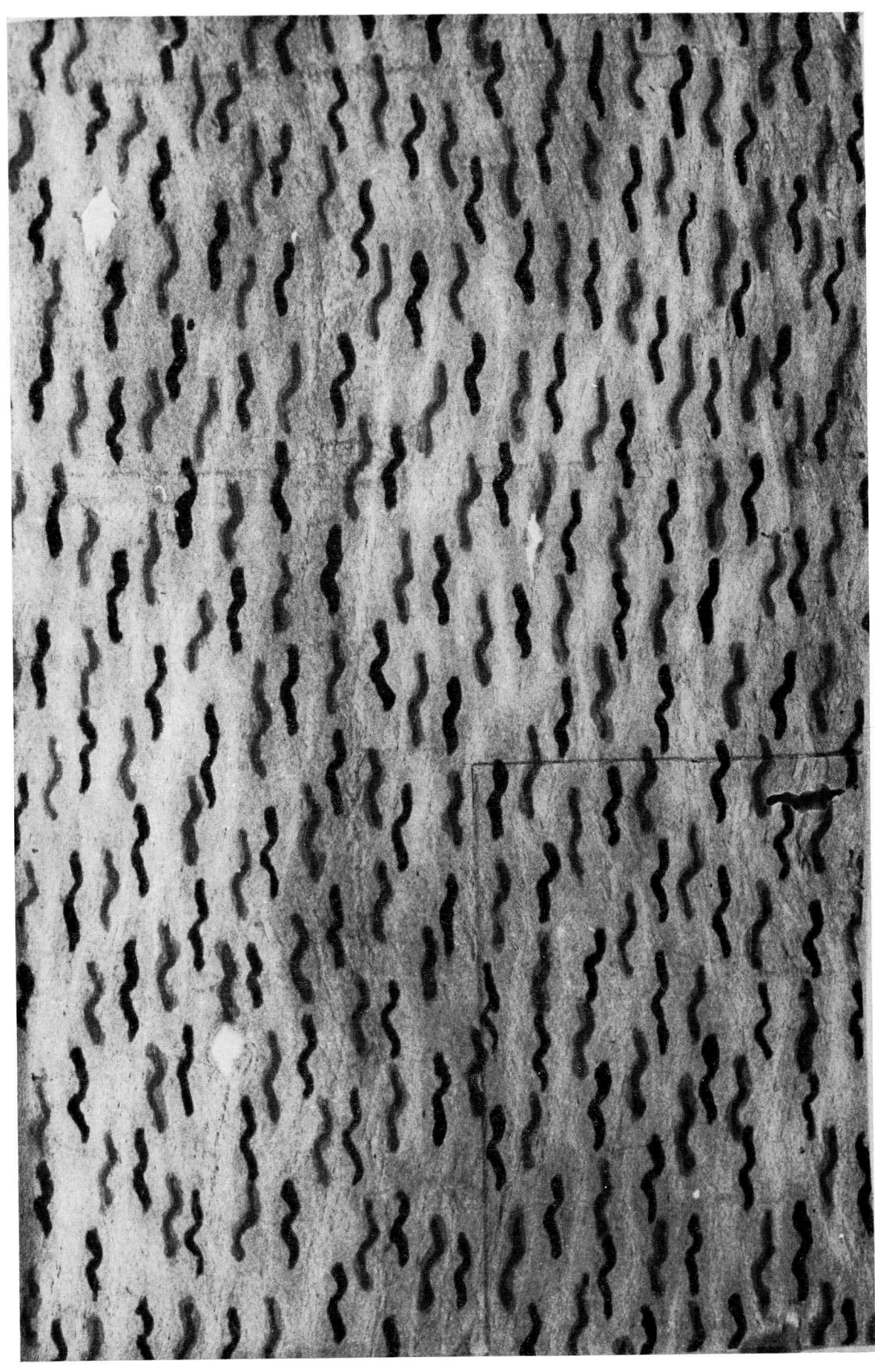

11. Reddish brown and black figures on natural.
Bound volume, p. 10. Actual size.

12. Reddish brown and black on natural.
Bound volume, p. 100. Actual size.

13. Reddish brown and black on yellowish ground.
Bound volume, p. 69. Actual size.

14. Reddish brown and black on natural.
Bound volume, p. 30. Actual size.

15. Reddish brown and black lines on natural.
Bound volume, p. 7. Actual size.

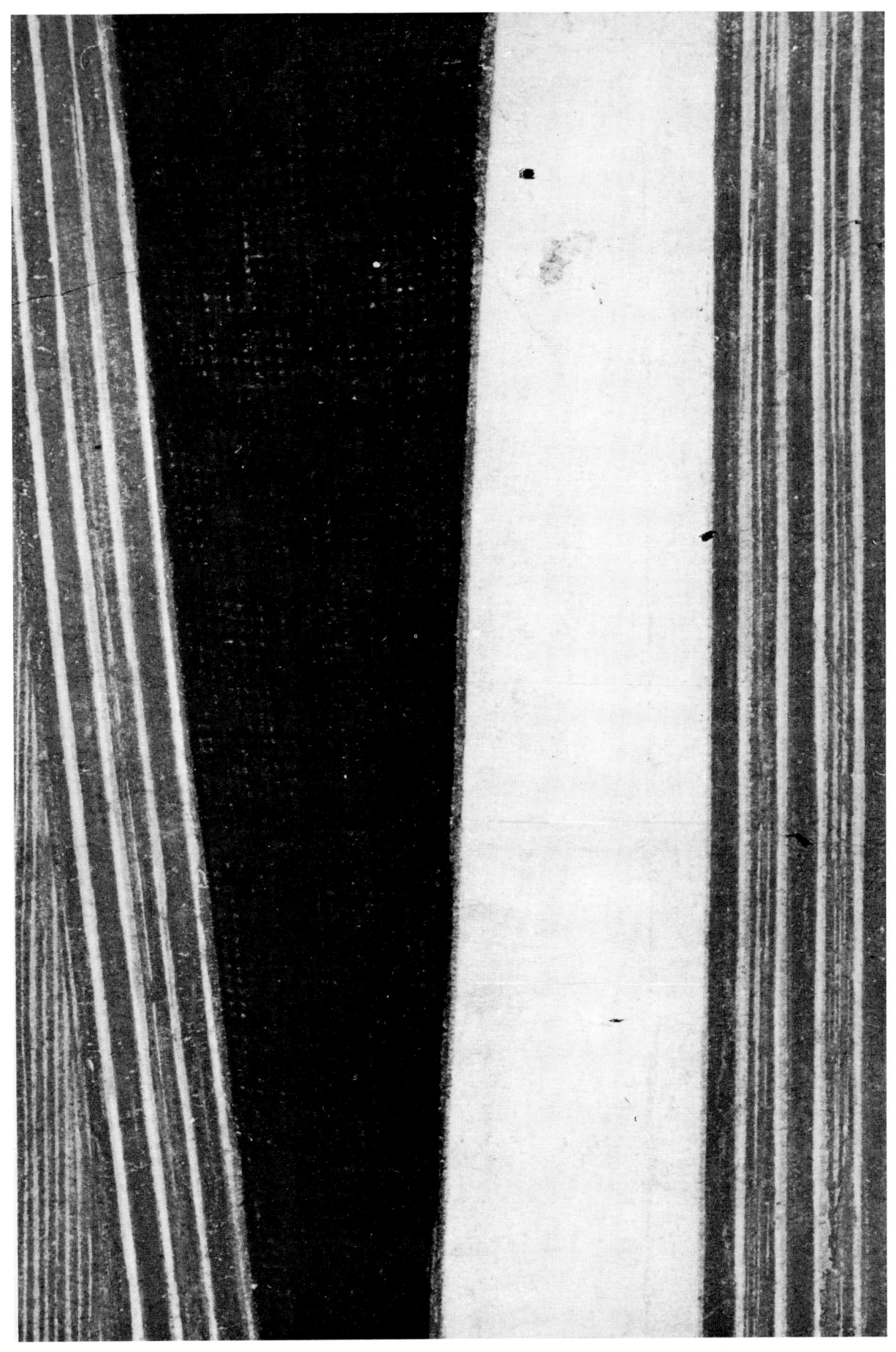

16.   Reddish brown and black on natural.
Bound volume, p. 27. Actual size.

17. Reddish brown and black on natural.
Bound volume, p. 8. Actual size.

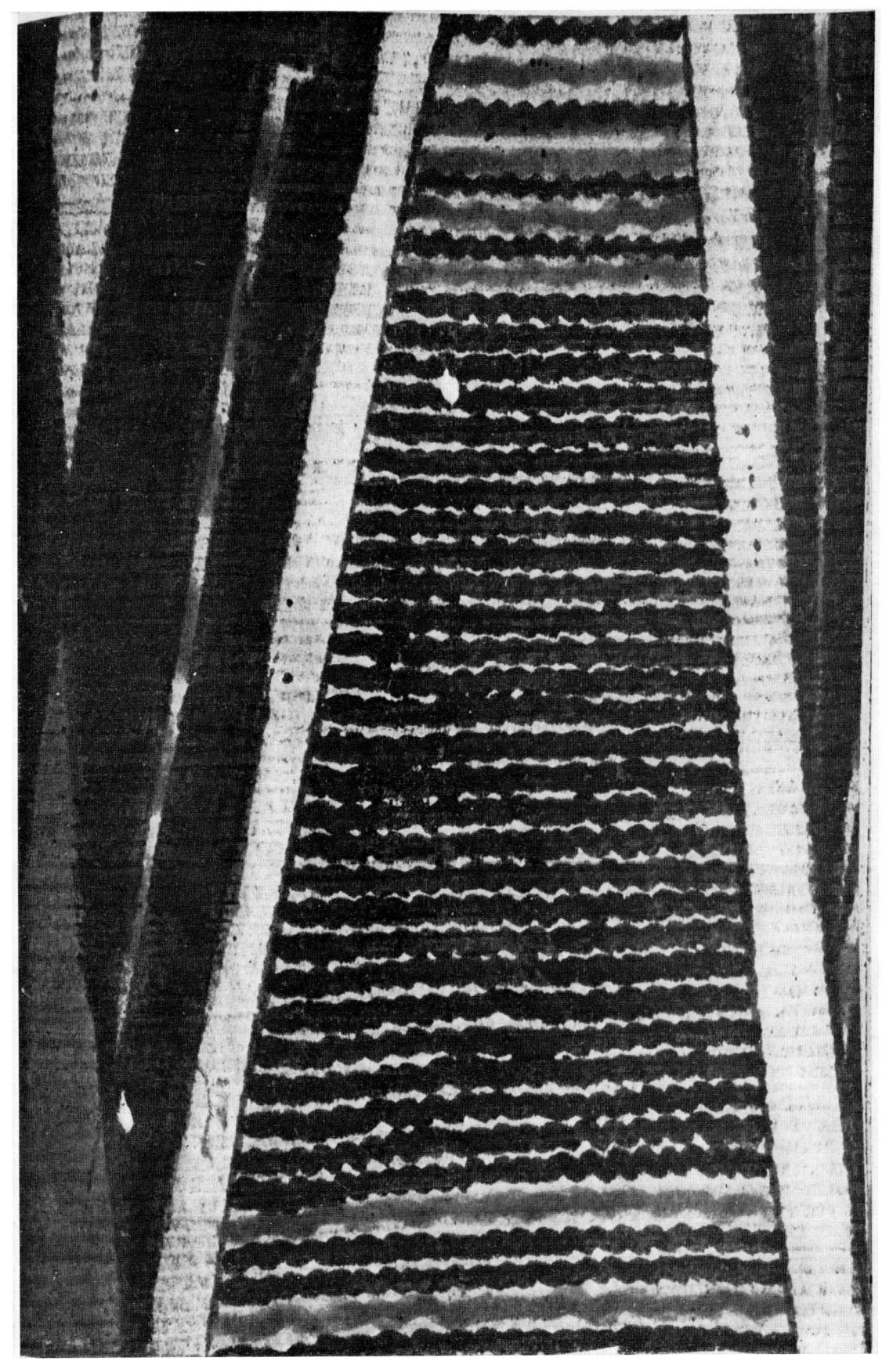

18. Reddish brown and black on natural. Bound volume, p. 65. Actual size.

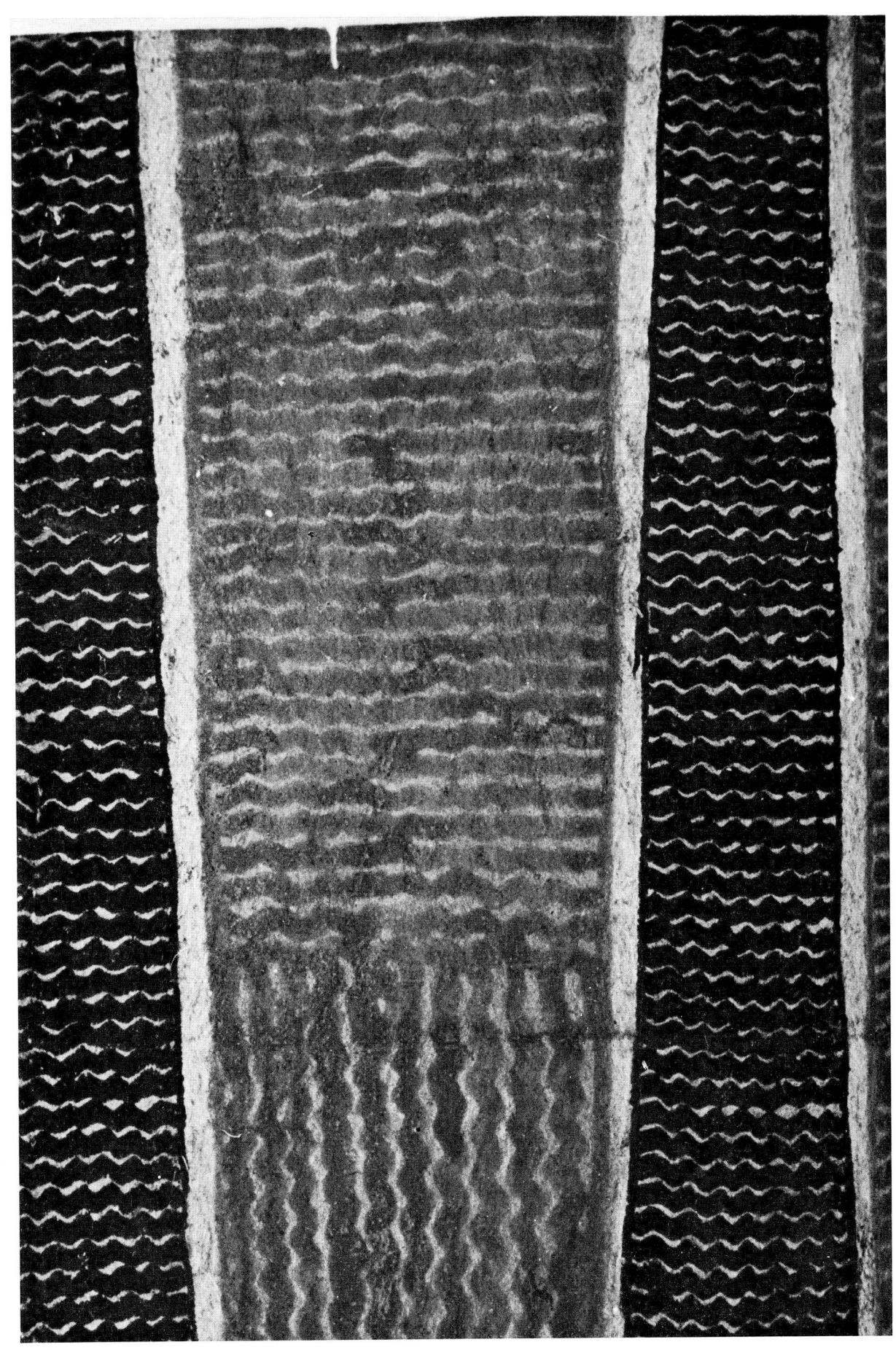

19. Reddish brown and black on yellowish ground.
Bound volume, p. 43. Actual size.

20. Reddish brown and black on natural.
Collected on Cook's third voyage. Three-quarters actual size.

21. Shades of reddish brown, yellow and black on natural.
Bound volume, p. 18. Actual size.

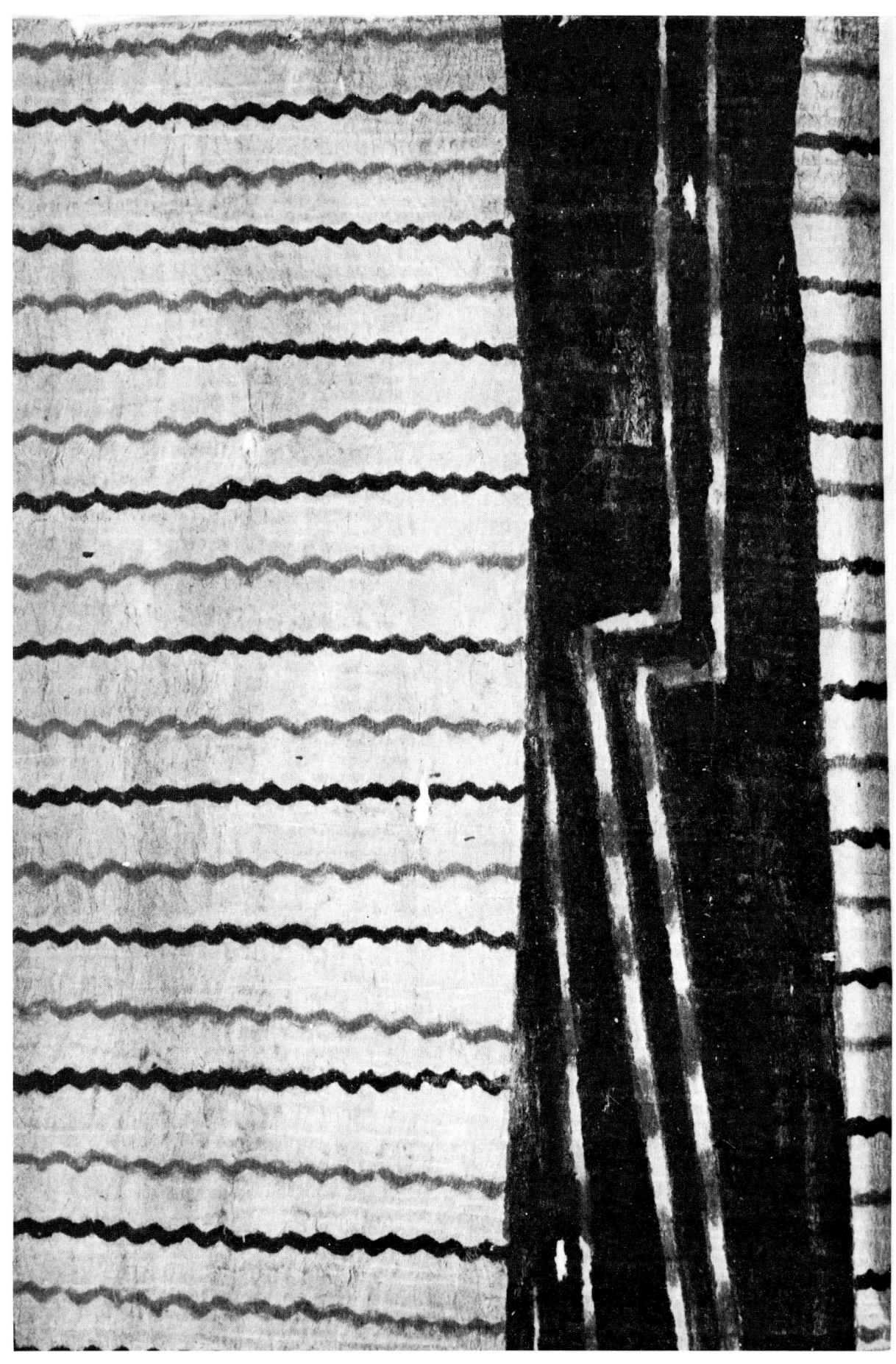

22. Reddish brown and black on natural.
Bound volume, p. 9. Actual size.

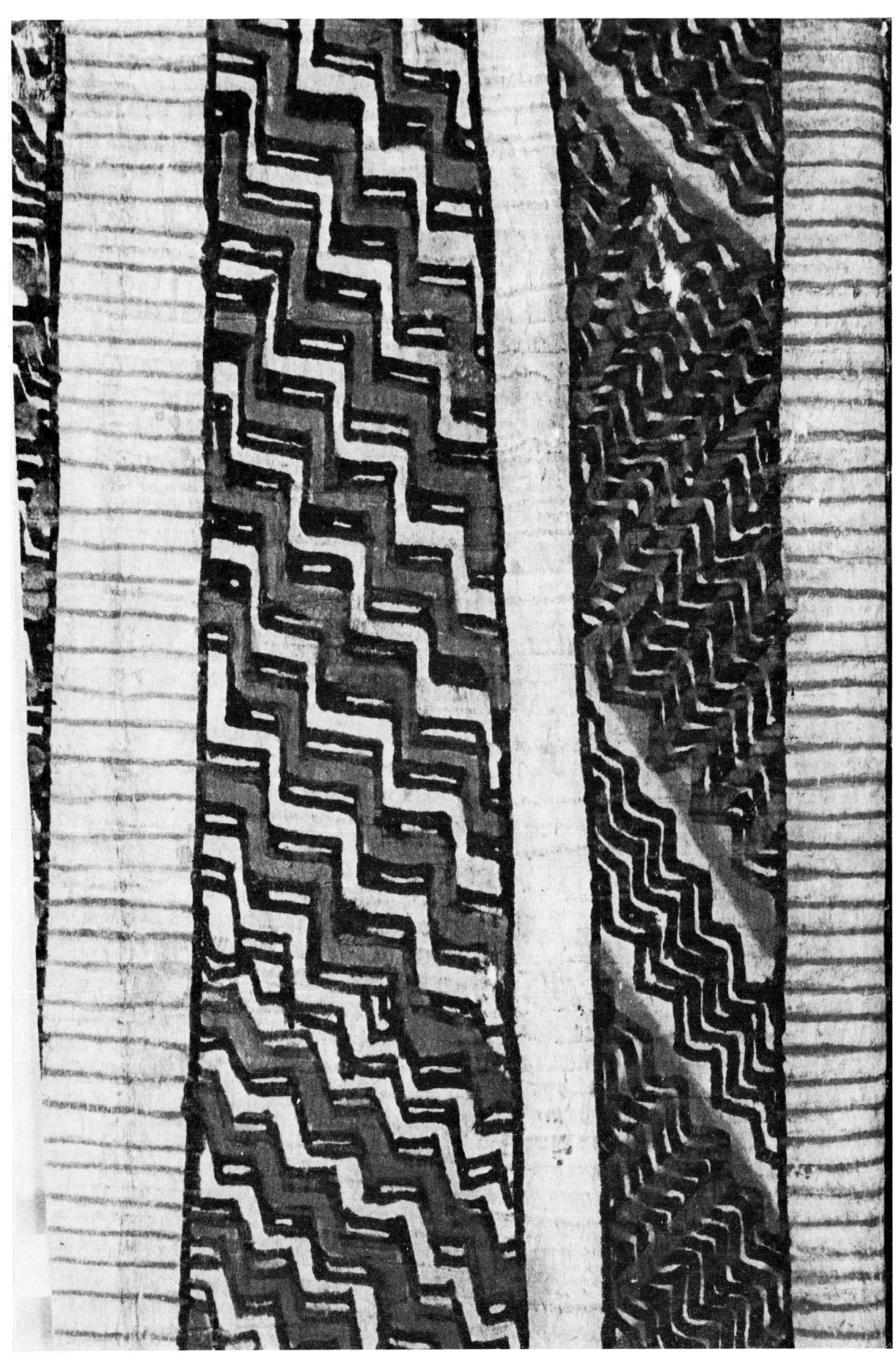

23. Reddish brown and black on natural.
Bound volume, p. 52. Actual size.

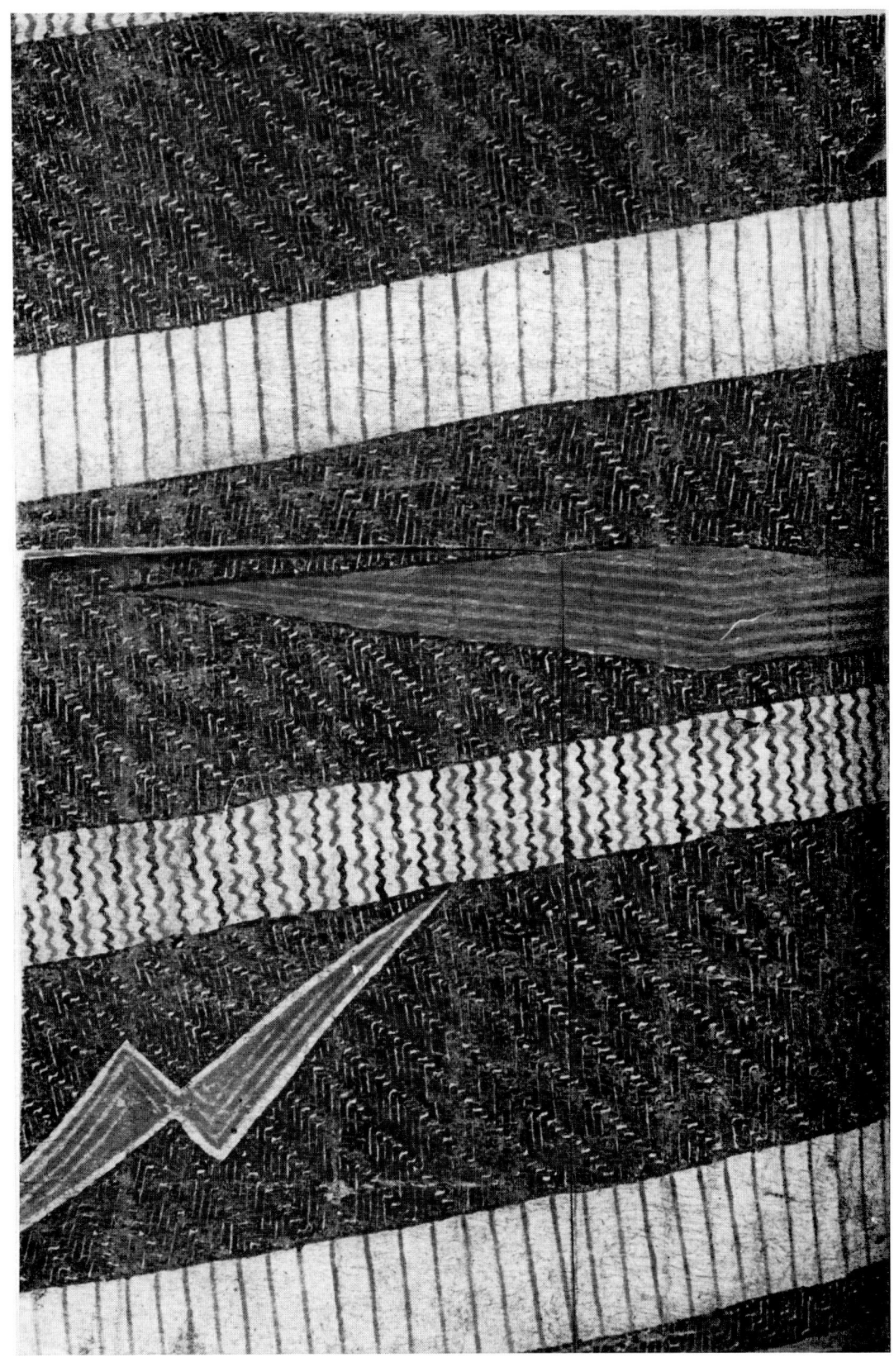

24.   Shades of reddish brown and black on natural.
Bound volume, p. 82. Actual size.

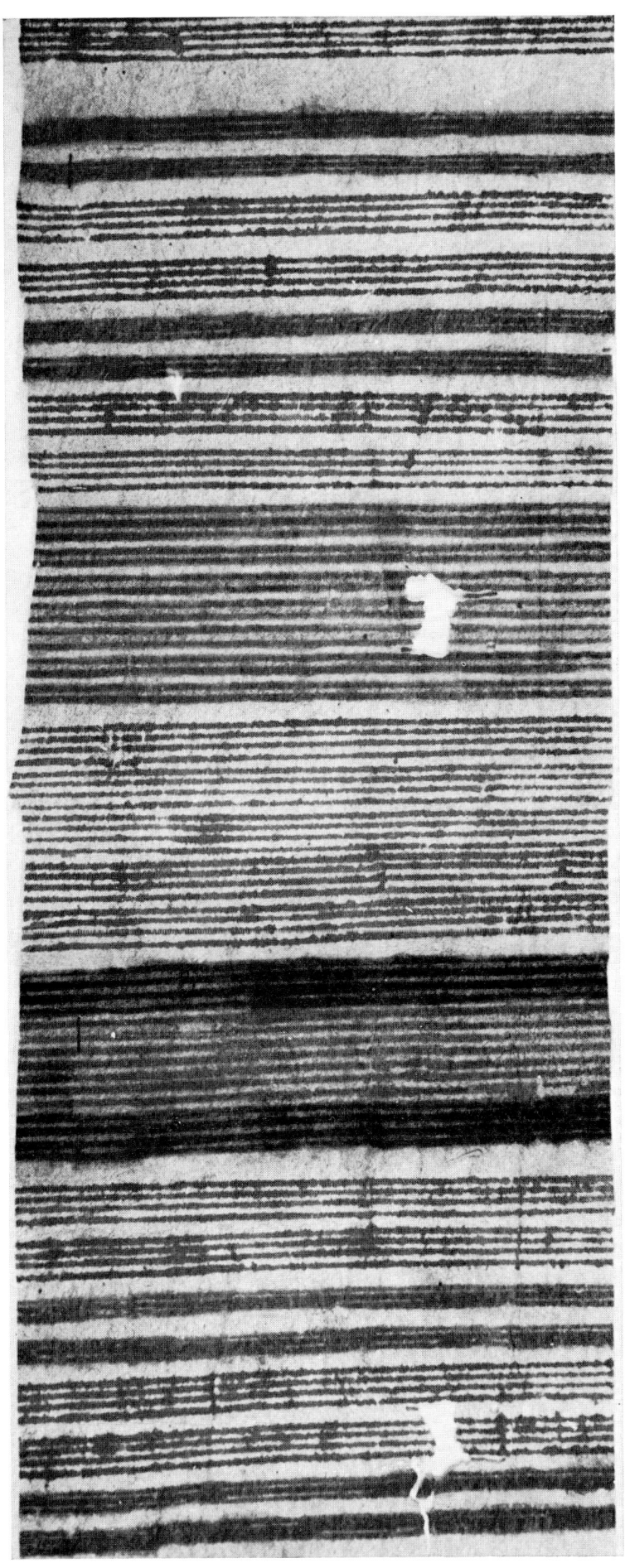

25. Shades of red and brown on natural.
Probably 18th century. Three-quarters actual size.

26. Reddish brown and black on natural.
Collected by Sir Edward Belcher before 1830. Probably 18th century.
Three-quarters actual size.

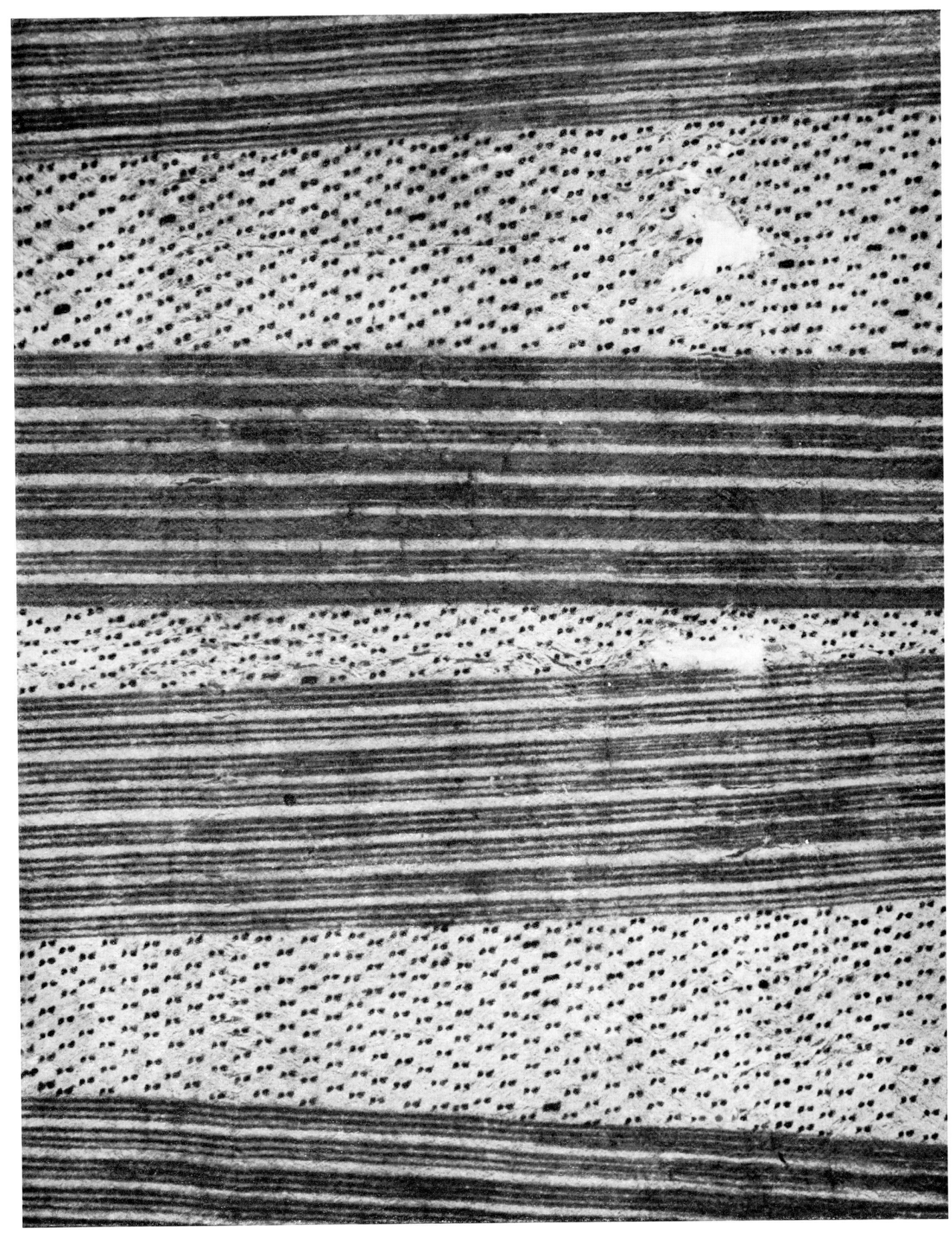

27. Reddish brown stripes and greenish black dots on natural. 18th-century in style. Ref. 2771. Three-quarters actual size.

28. Reddish brown and black on yellowish and natural.
Date unknown. Ref. 8851. Three-quarters actual size.

29. Reddish brown and charcoal on yellowish and ecru.
Date unknown. Three-quarters actual size.

30. Reddish brown.
Photographed through transmitted light to show watermark. Probably immersed in dye before final beating. From 'Mummy Cave'. Probably 19th century. Actual size.

31. Photographed through transmitted light to show textures and watermarks. 19th century. Actual size.

32. Photographed through transmitted light to show textures and watermarks. 19th century. Actual size.

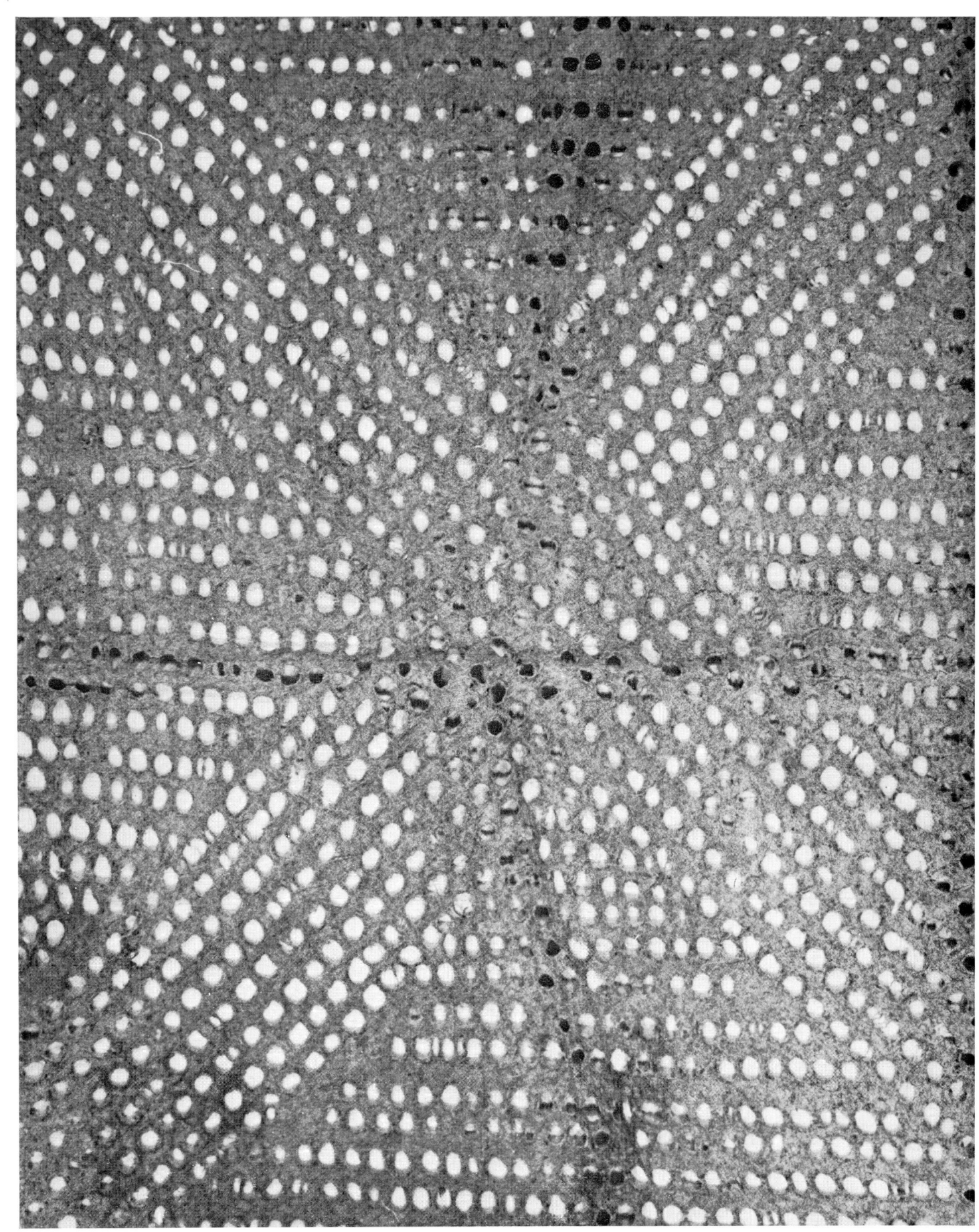

33.   Perforated or 'lace' bark cloth. Beige.
Probably 19th century. Three-quarters actual size.

35.   Reddish brown and black on gray.
Collected in 1802. Ref. P.A.S./E3164. Actual size.

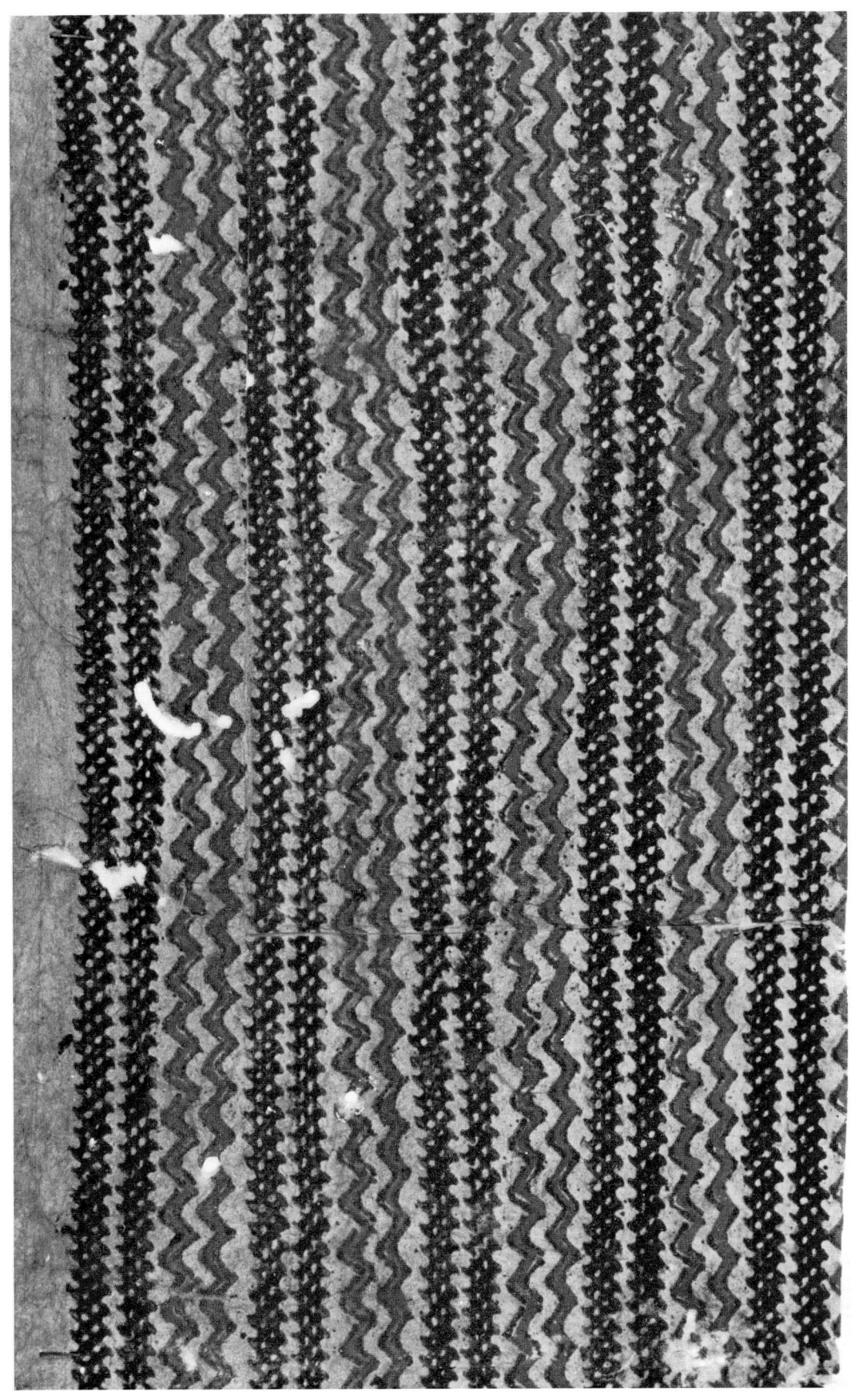

36. Reddish brown and black on ecru.
Ref. P.A.S./E3159. Actual size.

37. Red and black on yellowish ground. 19th century. Ref. 7785. Actual size.

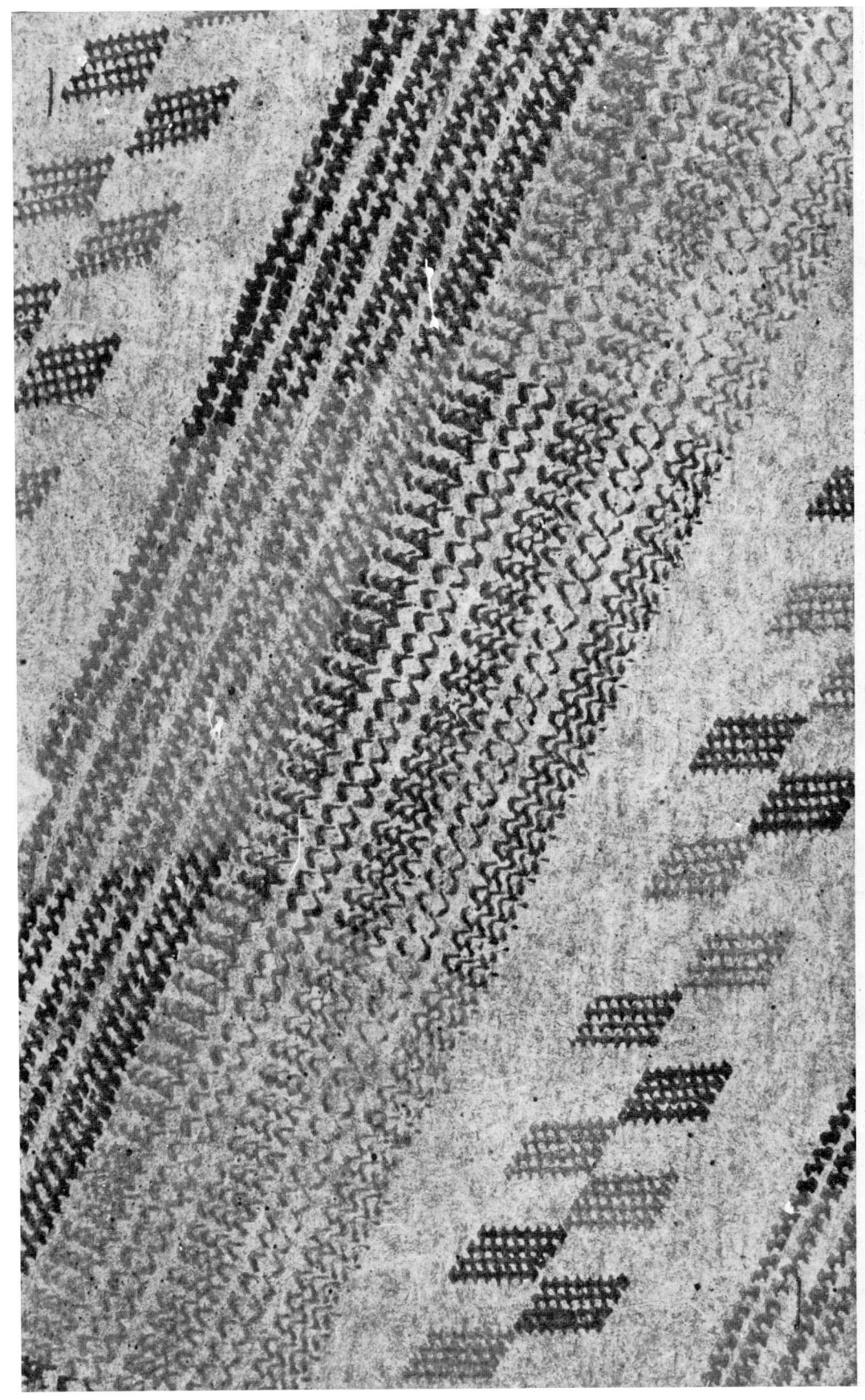

38. Red and black on yellowish ground.
19th century. Ref. 2316. Actual size.

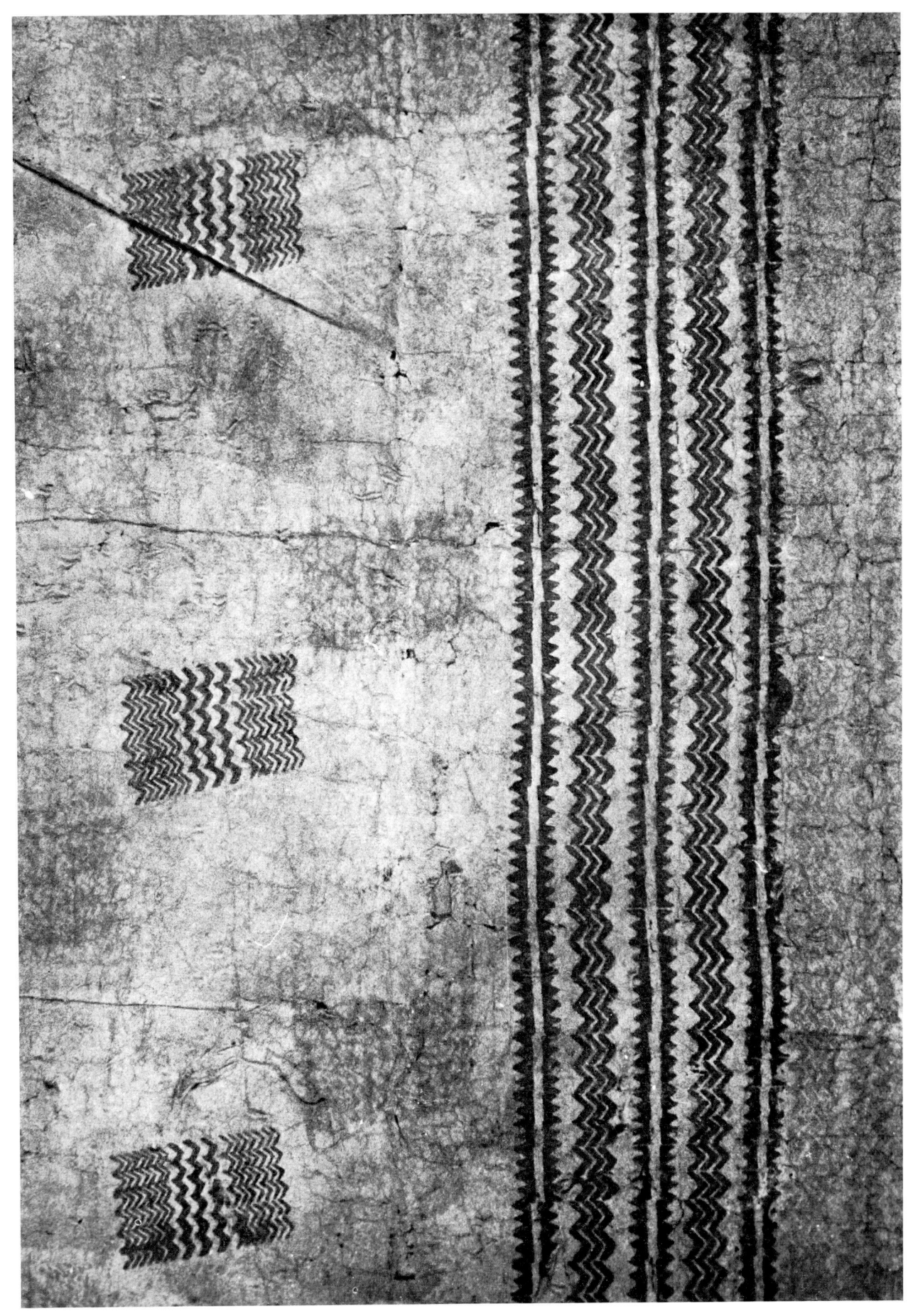

39. Light red and charcoal on yellowish ground.
19th century. Ref. 2477. Three-quarters actual size.

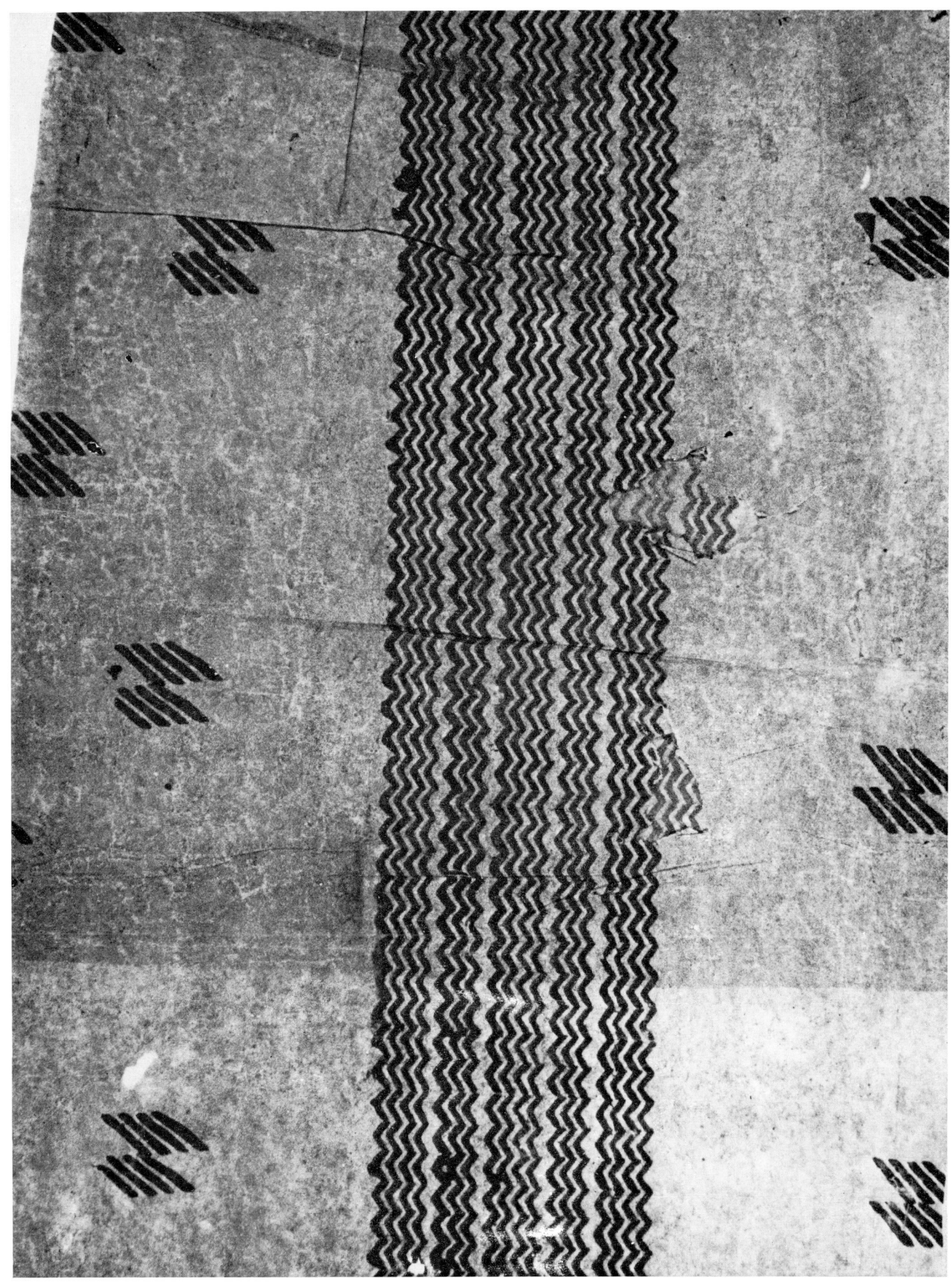

40. Black on brown.
19th century. Ref. 2761. Three-quarters actual size.

41. Charcoal on yellow.
19th century. Ref. 2548. Actual size.

42. Charcoal on salmon pink.
19th century. Ref. 2444. Actual size.

43. Charcoal on salmon pink.
19th century. Ref. 2329. Three-quarters actual size.

44. Charcoal on reddish brown.
19th century. Ref. C9653. Three-quarters actual size.

45. Reddish brown and black on blue.
19th century. Ref. 2443. Three-quarters actual size.

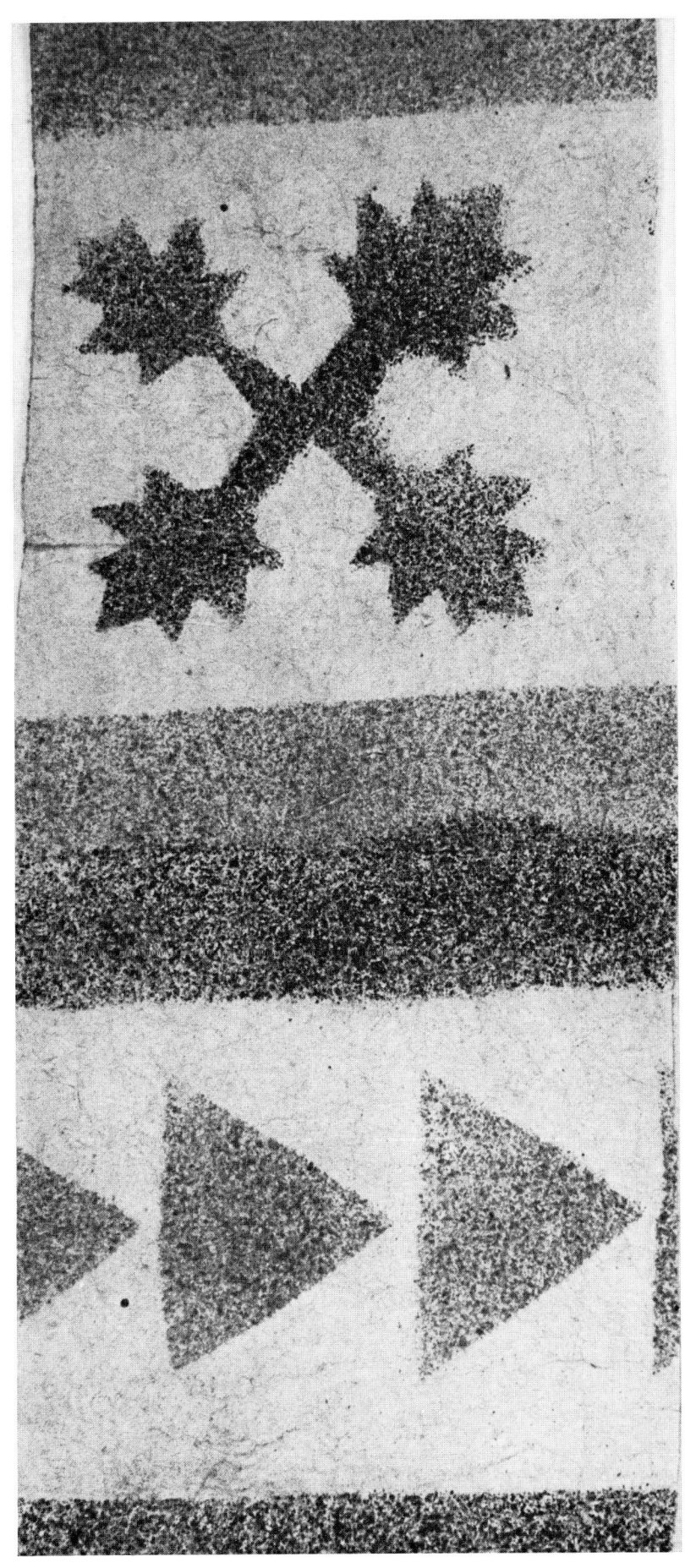

46. Reddish brown and gray on yellowish ground. 19th century. Ref. 3207. Three-quarters actual size.

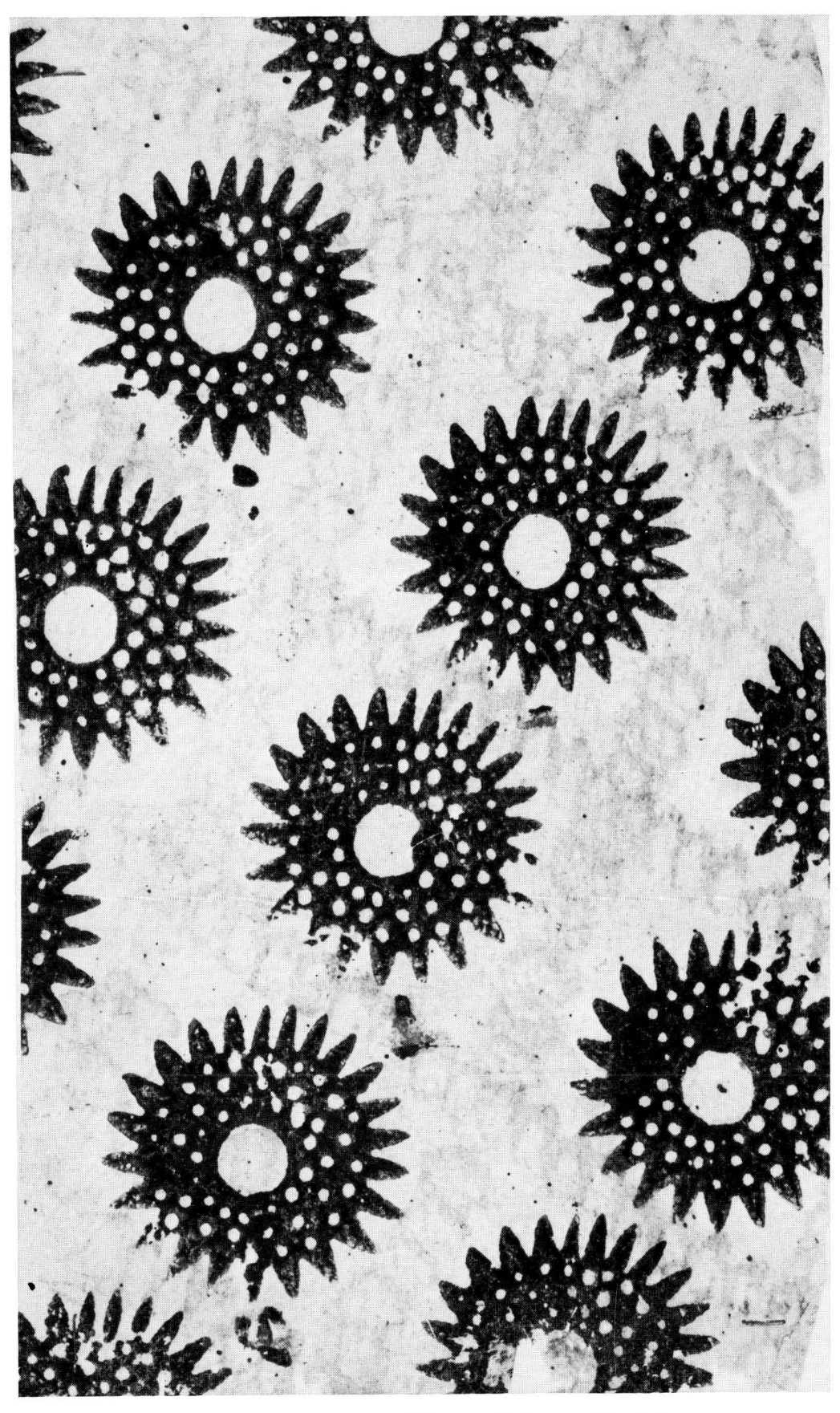

47. Pinkish and black on ecru. The so-called sea-urchin design. 19th century. Ref. 2395. Actual size.

48. Brown on beige.
19th century. Three-quarters actual size.

49. Shades of pink and charcoal.
19th century. Ref. 2397. Actual size.

50. Reddish brown and charcoal on ecru.
19th century. Ref. 2476. Three-quarters actual size.

51. Red and black on natural.
19th century. Ref. 2436. Three-quarters actual size.

52. Black on reddish brown and ecru.
19th century. Ref. 10.345. Three-quarters actual size.

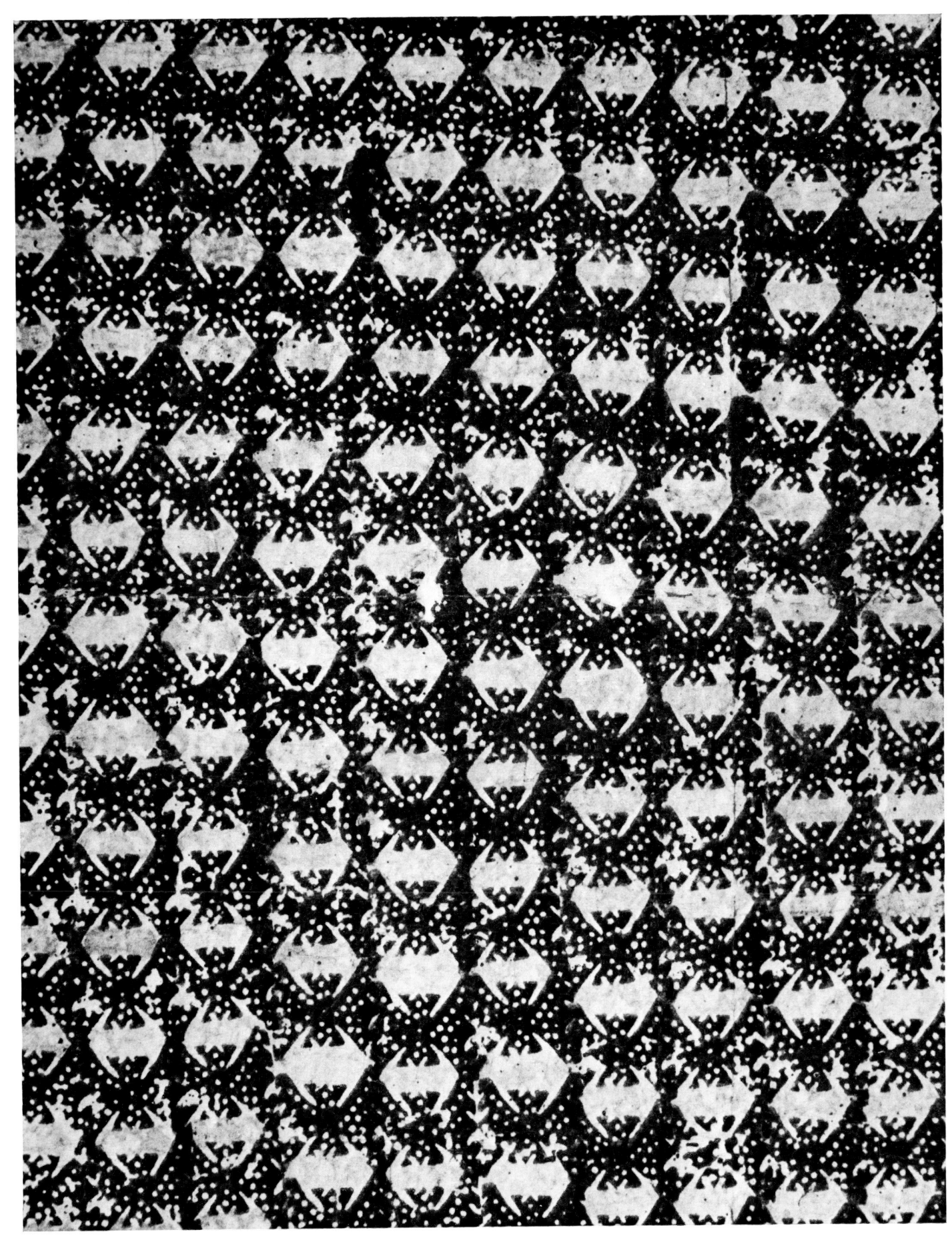

53. Black and pink.
19th century. Ref. 2469. Three-quarters actual size.

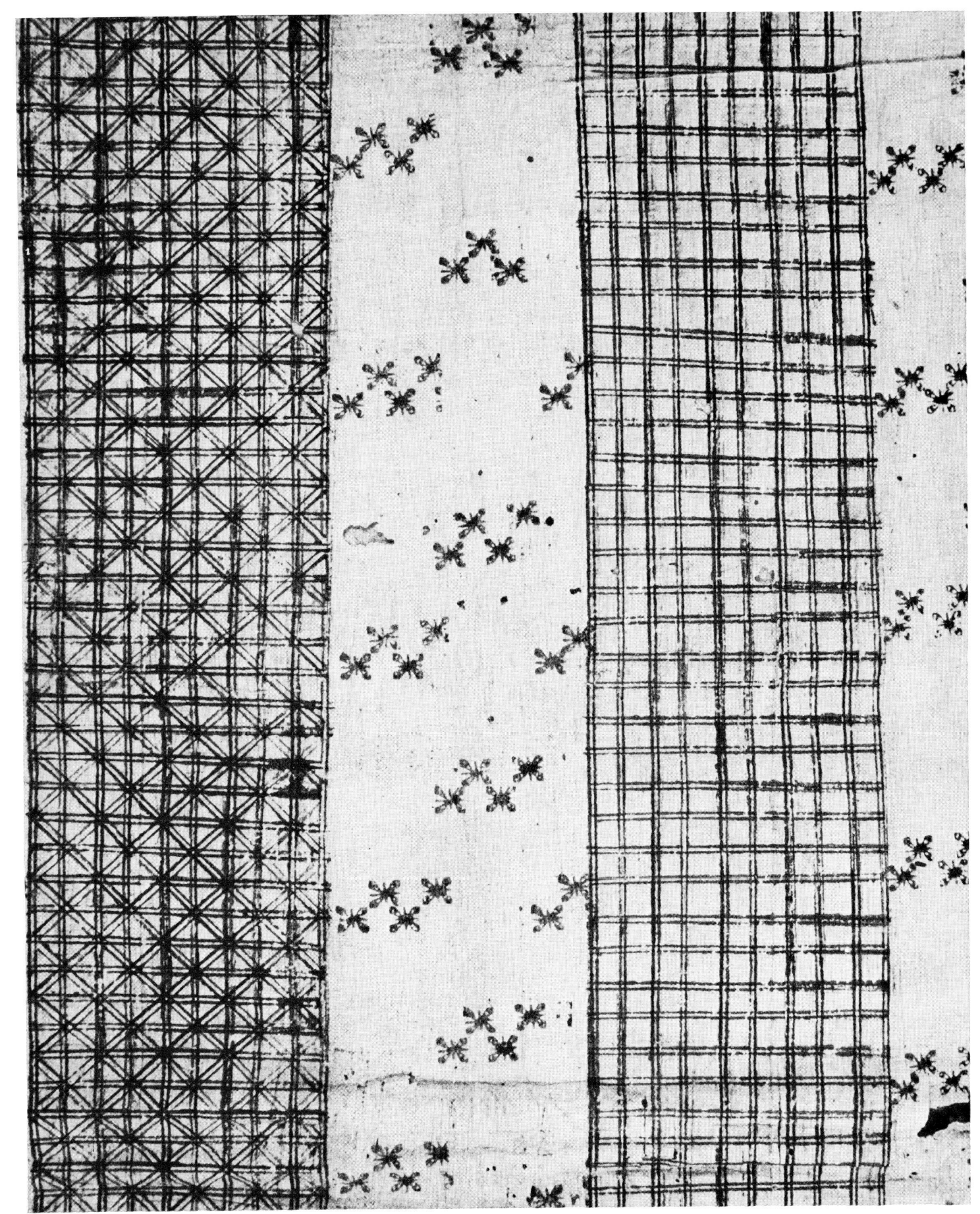

54. Charcoal on pink.
19th century. Ref. 2468. Three-quarters actual size.

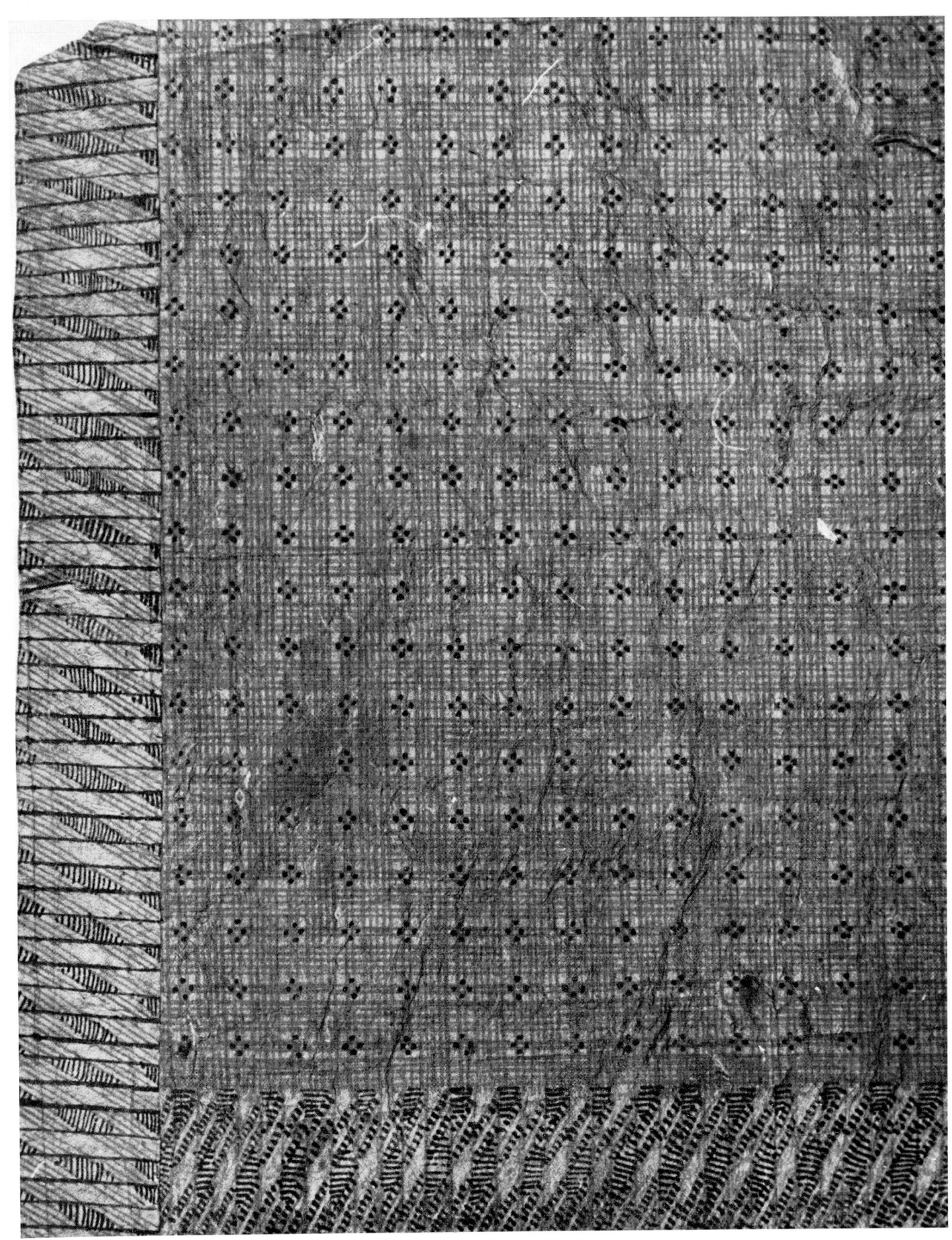

55. Red, brown and black on ecru.
19th century. Ref. B7917. Three-quarters actual size.